Social Science: A Very Short Introduction

VERY SHORT INTRODUCTIONS are for anyone wanting a stimulating and accessible way into a new subject. They are written by experts, and have been translated into more than 45 different languages.

The series began in 1995, and now covers a wide variety of topics in every discipline. The VSI library currently contains over 750 volumes—a Very Short Introduction to everything from Psychology and Philosophy of Science to American History and Relativity—and continues to grow in every subject area.

Very Short Introductions available now:

Available soon:

For more information visit our website

www.oup.com/vsi/

Alexander Betts

SOCIAL SCIENCE

A Very Short Introduction

OXFORD
UNIVERSITY PRESS

Great Clarendon Street, Oxford, OX2 6DP,
United Kingdom

Oxford University Press is a department of the University of Oxford.
It furthers the University's objective of excellence in research, scholarship,
and education by publishing worldwide. Oxford is a registered trade mark of
Oxford University Press in the UK and in certain other countries

Published in the United States of America by Oxford University Press
198 Madison Avenue, New York, NY 10016, United States of America

British Library Cataloguing in Publication Data

Data available

Library of Congress Control Number: 2024936330

ISBN 978-0-19-287182-4

Printed and bound by
CPI Group (UK) Ltd, Croydon, CR0 4YY

Links to third party websites are provided by Oxford in good faith and
for information only. Oxford disclaims any responsibility for the materials
contained in any third party website referenced in this work.

The manufacturer's authorised representative in the EU for product safety is Oxford
University Press España S.A. of el Parque Empresarial San Fernando de Henares,
Avenida de Castilla, 2 – 28830 Madrid (www.oup.es/en).

For Leo, Soxy, and Thea

Contents

Preface and acknowledgements

For many years, students have been telling me that they would like an accessible introduction to social science. This book is my attempt to deliver that, and to make it easier for people to study a subject I have been passionate about ever since I started doing social science subjects like geography and economics at school.

Today, there is a lot that is wrong with the world, and a range of urgent global, national, and local challenges, from climate change to poverty and pandemics. Social science cannot solve all of these problems by itself, but it can make a contribution to changing the world for the better. This is because it offers the tools for understanding and explaining human behaviour. And if we can make sense of people and powerful organizations' choices and actions, we may have the levers to change them.

We also live at a time when there are many competing claims about the world—from the media, corporate marketing, governments, and online conspiracy theories. Not all knowledge claims are equally valid. Social science can help us to critically engage with the claims that people make about the world; to assess whether claims about the social and economic world are valid or not, and also make sense of what underlies different worldviews.

Traditionally, social science has been taught by focusing on particular disciplines: political science, geography, sociology, anthropology, economics, law, and social psychology, for example. They each have their own strengths, core concepts, and methodologies. They also have a lot in common and many of the tools they offer are complementary and can be combined.

Given that today's big societal challenges often have political, economic, social, geographical, cultural, and legal dimensions, social scientists need to be able to work across disciplines. And that's why this book takes an interdisciplinary approach. In such a short book, I can't do justice to the richness of each of the disciplines, but I hope to enable readers to see the bigger picture of how the social sciences fit together, and to have confidence to think and communicate across disciplinary boundaries.

It is a really exciting time for social science, which is rapidly evolving. Technology and innovation are changing how social research is done. The digital revolution and the rise of artificial intelligence (AI) are not only changing human behaviour but also the way it is studied. Social scientists are increasingly working with the natural sciences and the humanities. Vital debates are taking place about how to make social science more equitable, diverse, and inclusive, and consider how social scientists can work in participatory ways with communities most directly affected by the research.

The book is aimed at anyone starting an undergraduate or masters course, as well as research students at the start of their PhD journey keen to get an overview of social science or wanting to understand how to design a social research project. But I also hope that it can still be useful for those later in their careers, and those earlier in their careers still at school. I have tried to write the book in a way that will be as relevant to those doing social science within an academic environment as for those doing social science for business or public policy, as well as interested citizens keen to make sense of how social science shapes our daily lives.

I have had to make choices on what to include and how to organize the book, which are informed by my own training and background. Not everyone will agree with all my choices. For example, there are different priorities and vocabularies in how social science is taught and undertaken in different regions of the world. However, I hope the book will be useful to you and offer a starting point for reflecting on and debating what it means to do interdisciplinary social science and use it to solve some of our most pressing societal challenges.

Many people have shaped my own intellectual journey as a social scientist, from school, through university, to the present day—and I'm grateful to everyone who has been part of that journey. That includes my inspiring colleagues and students in my own Department of International Development, at the Refugee Studies Centre where I have been able to do collaborative and interdisciplinary social science for nearly two decades, and at Brasenose College where every day offers an opportunity to learn across disciplines.

Serving as Associate Head of Oxford's Social Sciences Division, with responsibility for graduate student training, afforded me the opportunity to spend four years thinking about what social science training should look like for graduate students, enabling me to learn from researchers and students across our 14 different social science departments. Oxford is a great place to try new things and I've been supported to co-create research and education programmes that have an emphasis on collaborative and participatory mixed methods approaches to social science. I'm grateful to colleagues across my Refugee Economies Programme, the Refugee-Led Research Hub, and the SDG Impact Lab, who have helped me consider what interdisciplinary, inclusive, and impactful social science can and should be.

It is not only academics and students I have learned from, but also policy-makers, practitioners, and communities. Because most of my research focuses on the politics and economics of refugee policy, I have had the opportunity to work collaboratively with colleagues from international organizations such as the UN Refugee Agency and the World Economic Forum, governments around the world, and grassroots NGOs. I've learned incredible amounts from practitioners about what social science looks like, and when and how it can have impact, beyond academia. Working with refugees and people with lived experience of displacement has also deeply shaped how I think about social science—what is at stake in knowledge creation, the importance of participatory research methods, and the need to ensure that social science is seriously committed to equality, diversity, and inclusion.

It would be unfair to name the hundreds of people who have shaped my journey as a social scientist. But very specifically in relation to this book, I'd like to thank Imogene Haslam and Luciana O'Flaherty from OUP for their work to publish the book; Susan James Relly, with whom I co-convened the 'Oxford Minds: Reimaging the Future of Social Science' series during which I initially thought to write this book; Ed Brooks, with whom I've spent many hours exploring ideas that are discussed in the book, usually while running; and my wife Emily Kerr who contributed by being a sounding board for ideas, proofreading, and taking the kids camping to allow me to write.

List of illustrations

List of tables

Chapter 1
What is social science?

Human beings are complex creatures. The way they behave often seems random and unpredictable. But can we make sense of it? Are there patterns in the ways people live, interact, and build communities? And, if so, can we build theories that enable us to predict how people might act when faced with particular circumstances? If you've ever had a theory about why people sometimes act in the ways that they do, you are part way to becoming a social scientist.

Social science is the study of human behaviour, and the resulting outcomes. Behaviour can refer to many things. It can be about people's preferences and choices—when and why do they select one alternative over another, whether that's ice cream versus fruit, or a red political party over a blue one. It may be about their actions—when do they do things that are regarded as kind and compassionate, from litter-picking to working as a volunteer? It can be about their interactions—what makes them decide to cooperate or compete with others in a particular task, whether that's children with toys or two businesses?

Importantly, social science is concerned with society—the way people live together in communities and interact. You won't find a social science theory of Queen Victoria or Beyoncé. That's because each individual is far too complicated to theorize, and you cannot easily build an explanation for human behaviour by observing just one individual. You would have no basis on which to claim that that individual's experience was representative of a wider pattern. So, while individuals are often the focus of the humanities and the natural sciences, social scientists generally focus on observing and understanding the behaviour of groups.

Social science matters because it can provide sources of evidence that inform decision-making across business, government, and society. Almost any social question can be explored using the tools offered by social science. How do countries get richer? What determines children's educational outcomes? How do diseases spread? Why do people vote for particular political parties? What shapes race and gender inequality? What makes people give up smoking? If we understand the causes and consequences of actions, we can change them. With insights from social science, policy-makers, chief executives, community leaders, consumers, and citizens may be persuaded to change their behaviour. This can make a difference in areas as diverse as addressing climate change, shaping electoral outcomes, fighting pandemics, ending wars, and alleviating poverty.

One of the things that makes social science so adaptable, and such a powerful tool for understanding the world, is that it can be applied to different types of social actor (units of analysis): individuals, families, networks, organizations, firms, and nation-states, for example. Why do some people gamble, eat unhealthy foods, or hold racist beliefs? How do families allocate household tasks, raise children effectively, or manage grief? How do companies weigh profit against environment sustainability, decide to invest in innovation, or adopt policies to address unequal pay between women and men? Why do countries sign international treaties, commit human rights atrocities, or transition from authoritarianism to democracy?

What distinguishes social science from mere speculation or from most journalism, is the attempt to answer these questions using systematic and rigorous methods. This traditionally involves two key tasks: describing and explaining. How do people behave? Why do they behave that way? Description can be challenging because it is not usually possible to speak to every single person of interest. Instead, social scientists may need to collect or use information from a sample of the group they are interested in. But they will need to know that the sample is representative of the larger group. For example, if we want to know how frequently all university students in Europe play sport, it would be unrealistic to ask all 18.5 million students across the continent. So we could instead use data from a subset of students that approximates the characteristics of the larger group.

Explanation can be challenging because most behaviours and outcomes have lots of determinants. They are caused by many different factors. Again, if we wanted to know why some university students play more sport than others, this might be influenced by sex, ethnicity, economic circumstances, health, or other responsibilities, for example. Attributing an observed outcome (e.g. low levels of sports participation among students from lower socio-economic groups) to a particular cause (the cost of being part of the team or lack of time due to needing to work part-time) relies upon being able to demonstrate that without that particular factor, the observed outcome would not otherwise have taken place.

Social science is a vast, diverse, and contested field. Traditionally, social science has been an umbrella term for a series of academic disciplines, including anthropology, political science, economics, sociology, geography, social psychology, and law. Each discipline has its own object of study (culture, politics, law, and so forth), specialist knowledge, methods, theories and concepts, and terminology. But these disciplines have a lot in common in how they think about questions, theory, and methods. They borrow from one another and have a significant shared vocabulary. They are also frequently brought together in order to respond to questions that go beyond any one particular discipline.

The most complex societal challenges—from pandemics to climate change—transcend any one discipline, requiring interdisciplinary approaches. They involve collaboration across the social sciences, and also require that social science works with the sciences and the humanities. While students continue to be trained within disciplines, a growing proportion of ground-breaking and impactful social science research is interdisciplinary. And there is a need for students, and practitioners from government and business, to have a sound understanding of 'social science' as distinct from any one particular discipline.

There are many different ways to be a social scientist, whether within or across disciplines. Some use quantitative methods, others use qualitative methods, many combine both. Quantitative methods use statistical data, drawn from survey questionnaires, experiments that introduce a particular intervention to one group but not to another comparable group, or pre-existing datasets. Such approaches aspire to create evidence that is objective, comparable, and representative for the population of interest. Qualitative methods work with non-numerical data, and seek to interpret human behaviour, including through guided conversations, observation of people's cultures and habits known as ethnography, or the analysis of text or visual media. Mixed methods try to combine the best of both, integrating context-specific depth with representative breadth.

Not all social science is focused on practical problem-solving by describing and explaining the world as it is. A significant part is engaged in critique, including of the knowledge produced by other social scientists and used by government and business. Critical social science seeks to make visible the power relations, vested interests, and dominant ideas that underlie the status quo. These approaches are especially valuable given that lots of knowledge—including social scientific knowledge—is created within a particular political and historical environment. It is shaped by the gendered, racialized, and social class context within which it is produced and given legitimacy. For example, some dominant ideas in social science have their origins in colonialism. A range of approaches, from critical race theory to feminism, seek to uncover how social knowledge and power interact.

A growing part of social science is also interested in so-called normative questions: how the world should be. Rather than just understanding and explaining how it is; how can we know what a better society would look like? Such approaches draw heavily on insights from ethics and philosophy, but sometimes combine them with more conventional social science methods to identify transformative visions for rethinking and reimagining a more just and equitable world. What proportion of a country's national income should it spend on international development aid? Do states have an obligation to admit refugees onto their territory? What intergenerational obligations do people have towards not-yet born people, in areas such as climate change? While such normative questions have often been marginalized by social science, or regarded as more appropriately addressed within the humanities, it is impossible to conceive of a transformative vision for the social sciences that does not also take into account the tools and methods of normative theory.

There are no perfect social science methods. The art of being a good social scientist is finding the best available methods to fit your particular question. The aim is to ensure that the chosen methods are sufficiently justifiable to make the findings from the research persuasive enough to withstand the scrutiny of other social scientists and, ideally, to also influence the decision-making of government, business, and society in ways that create a better and more just world.

Why this book?

The aim of this book is to provide an accessible introduction to
social science. But this begs the question of why 'social science' as
a whole, rather than, for example, addressing each of the
different social science disciplines (e.g. sociology or economics)
separately. Surely, within 35,000 words it is impossible to do
justice to the diverse array of different disciplines? Indeed, my aim
is not to comprehensively cover all social science disciplines, but
rather to introduce social science as an interdisciplinary area.

Interdisciplinary social science is growing, partly based on the
recognition that complex societal challenges cannot be addressed
from a single disciplinary perspective. While specific disciplines
serve academic purposes such as the organization of specialist
training, the creation of communities for organized scholarly
debate, and the advancement of specialized knowledge, they
struggle to grapple with the major global challenges of our time.
Climate change, pandemics, wars, migration, mental health,
inequality, transnational organized crime, for example, all require
the insight of social science research to inform creative solutions,
but solutions transcend disciplinary boundaries. These grand
challenges necessitate collaboration across disciplines—both
within and beyond the social sciences. They are political,
economic, social, cultural, and legal. They also require a coherent
basis for dialogue across the social sciences, the natural sciences,
and the humanities.

The contemporary world needs a generation of scholars and
practitioners who are conversant in the language of
interdisciplinary social science, and who have the ability to
engage in dialogue beyond their specialist training. It requires that
an economist can speak to an anthropologist, that humanities
and science students know some social science, and that
practitioners in business and government have enough familiarity

with social science to lead research and work effectively with researchers. Not everyone has to be able to do everything, but shared familiarity with a common set of ideas and debates is essential.

With that in mind, the book has three main aims and audiences—educational, collaborative, and participatory. First, in terms of *education*, the book will serve as an introduction for students studying or interested in understanding social science. Many teaching programmes at university are now in the 'social sciences' rather than specific disciplines. Students entering such programmes, whether as undergraduate or graduate students, may wish to be able to see the wood for the trees, situating their more specialized studies with the broader landscape of social science. Others, who specialize or major in non-social science subjects, may also want an accessible way to understand the social sciences.

Second, in terms of *collaboration*, a growing proportion of research and research funding transcends disciplines. Barriers to effective collaboration often include a lack of common training, language, or awareness of other people's roles and competencies. But the rewards for effective interdisciplinary collaboration to address global challenges are potentially enormous, in terms of impact on people and planet, and the potential for academic innovation. For example, during COVID-19, social scientists were able to work effectively with medical scientists and government in order to understand behaviour questions such as face coverings and vaccine hesitancy. By making accessible key ideas that are common across the social sciences, the book offers a resource that might facilitate working productively across professional and disciplinary boundaries.

Third, in terms of *participation*, the book aims to offer an introduction to members of the public, from all walks of life and professional backgrounds. Ideas drawn from the social sciences are pervasive across society, in the media and in politics. To engage with current affairs relies upon being able to understand and scrutinize the ways in which social science is used and abused in public life. From political speeches to articles in *The Economist* and the *New York Times*, theories, correlations, and causal relationships derived from social science are frequently evoked to advance argument. Being able to participate meaningfully in public life as a citizen necessitates a basic understanding of social science. Moreover, social science research does not only take place in universities. It is also undertaken across a range of other professions. Government, business, and civil society organizations undertake social science research. In 2015, the British Council undertook a survey of over 1,700 'leaders' from around the world and found that, of those with degrees, 44 per cent had taken an undergraduate social science degree. This book offers an accessible introduction for time-scarce practitioners keen to get an overview of social science, for, say, public policy or consultancy.

Of course, social science is a diverse and contested field. Although my own view is that the social sciences have more in common than that which divides them, I cannot possibly reduce social science to a single common language. Disciplines often have their own terms and concepts for good reasons of precision and clarity, and different geographical areas sometimes use different terminology to describe similar ideas. Some differences are cosmetic, others relate to boundaries (such as, whether history is a social science). The challenge is to find the most inclusive and accessible terms that are as applicable as possible across disciplines and regions. My aim is not to change or critique existing disciplinary language, but to facilitate dialogue and effective communication across disciplines within the social sciences, wherever possible. Where there are common or shared concepts I will aim to highlight this, and where there are concepts that are specific to particular disciplines, I will explain the reasons for this.

This book therefore aims to draw together the common elements that comprise interdisciplinary social science, and make them accessible to a wide readership across universities, schools, businesses, government, and society. It will provide the basic tools for doing and interpreting social science, and equip readers with the ability to navigate the social sciences and make informed judgements relating to the strengths and weaknesses of particular approaches to social science research. Throughout, the book will showcase examples of inspiring and impactful social science that is improving lives and changing the world for the better.

Disciplines and interdisciplinarity

Social science has historically been organized into academic disciplines (such as sociology or economics). A discipline is a field of study, created to subdivide knowledge into specialist areas. They serve to organize teaching and research, especially within an academic context. Disciplines have existed in loose form since the earliest universities. While centres of learning have emerged in many regions of the world, the idea of the university began as a European concept. The early curricula at the first 11th- and 12th-century universities—Oxford, Paris, and Bologna, for example—focused on mathematics, theology, law, and *Literae Humaniores* (classical languages, philosophy, and history), enabling shared learning. The language of 'disciplines' was used from the mid-19th century, to catalogue and archive the output of scholars, and then to enable the expansion of the curriculum following the secularization of universities, with a vast array of new disciplines emerging and proliferating over time. Many of the social science disciplines developed a distinctive identity in the first half of the 20th century.

Disciplines have many advantages. They enable specialization, ensuring that research and education are underpinned by deep understanding of a particular area, and that training has sufficient depth. They create academic community, enabling like-minded researchers to work with and teach alongside people thinking about similar topics. This clustering can contribute to innovation, as leading scholars work together to push the boundaries of disciplinary knowledge. Disciplines also support high standards. When researchers publish their work in discipline-specific academic journals or present their work to learned societies organized along disciplinary lines, they are subjected to peer review by scholars with relevant expertise and shared norms, helping to maintain rigorous standards.

However, disciplines can also have disadvantages. They may be conservative and slow to adapt to new research questions. Instead of responding to the challenges and needs of society, they may have an inward-looking focus on incrementally building on debates within the discipline. As the French philosopher Michel Foucault argued, disciplines may be hierarchically organized in ways that ossify norms of valid knowledge, excluding and disqualifying knowledge that does not fit the disciplinary norms recognized by leading academic journals and learned societies. Perhaps most importantly, as previously highlighted, real-world challenges usually transcend disciplinary boundaries, requiring insights from across a range of theories and methods derived from across, or even beyond, the social sciences.

Each of the main social science disciplines can be characterized by their distinctive methods, concepts, and questions. In practice, disciplines are internally diverse and scholars regularly borrow ideas from other disciplines. The boundaries between disciplines are not always rigid. Table 1 gives a simplified summary of some of the characteristics of the main social science disciplines. The summary in the table is, of course, an oversimplification and does not do justice to the complexity and depth of each discipline, but it hopefully offers an accessible way in which those new to social science can get a sense of the distinctive focus and comparative advantage of each discipline.

For example, law is sometimes seen as a social science, and sometimes not. Legal scholars use legal methods to interpret what

Table 1. Simplified summary of the main social science disciplines

Discipline	Methods	Concepts	Question
Law	Interpretation	Rights & duties	What are the rules?
Political science	Eclectic	Power & interests	What explains variation in systems of governance?
Anthropology	Ethnography	Culture	How can we understand lived experience?
Sociology	Eclectic	Institutions & identity	What explains social change and behaviour?
Economics	Econometrics & Randomized Control Trials (RCTs)	Efficiency	What explains resource allocation choices?
Social psychology	Experiments	Attitudes	How do people perceive the world?
Human geography	Geographic information systems (GIS) & cartography	Space & place	How can we understand the relationship between physical and human phenomena?

the law (whether derived from statutes or past cases) means for contemporary cases. Among its many concepts of interest, it is concerned with assigning rights and duties. Some disciplines have distinctive methodologies. For example, anthropology has ethnography—a series of qualitative methods that rely heavily on participant observation (participating in the activities of the people being studied as part 'insider' and part 'outsider')—as a means to understand people's lived experiences and culture on their own terms. Economics is distinctive for its use of quantitative methods, often important from other disciplines such as statistics, computer science, and experimental psychology. Meanwhile, other disciplines—such as political science and sociology—have very specific central concepts (including power and interests, and institutions and identity), but draw methods eclectically from across the social sciences.

Students and researchers often select their primary disciplines based on both the kinds of questions they are interested in and their aptitude for using particular research methods. One of the great things about the social sciences is that they are sufficiently diverse that there is something for almost everyone. People who like statistics may enjoy economics, people who like maps may appreciate geography, and people who like spending time interacting with people in unfamiliar contexts may be budding anthropologists.

But to really solve the world's major challenges, we have to go beyond disciplines. And that is why interdisciplinarity has emerged as one of the most important themes in the social sciences. In my own research, I take a challenge-led perspective. I focus on refugee rights—trying to understand when and under what conditions people fleeing war and authoritarian government gain access to sanctuary and support. I mainly use political science—my primary area of training—to understand why government responses vary. But I also use economics to explain variation in the welfare outcomes of refugees; why some are better off than others. And I also need some familiarity with law to understand countries' legal obligations towards refugees, and anthropology to have insights into the range of cultural contexts in which I do much of my research in refugee camps and cities around the world. It would be impossible to master every discipline myself, but working across disciplines has been central to answering the questions I am interested in and that I believe matter for people's lives.

Interdisciplinarity can be about 'multi-disciplinarity', whereby people from different disciplines come together to work on shared projects but stick to their areas of disciplinary expertise, or 'trans-disciplinarity', creating new methods and theories that transcend disciplinary boundaries. It can also be about working across disciplines *within* the social sciences or *beyond* the social sciences with the humanities and the natural sciences, for example. An increasing number of research challenges now rely on interdisciplinary that is both within and beyond. Indeed, interdisciplinary social science has been described by behavioural scientist Anastasia Buyalskaya and colleagues as entering a 'golden age'. The big data revolution, new global challenges, and innovation in science and technology are creating new ways to do social science. Emerging approaches such as behavioural science and human data science, which draw upon insights from neuroscience and psychology, are generating alternative ways to understand society, including through new methods such as lab and field experiments. These emerging approaches are not just used by university academics but also by business and government to understand the behaviour of consumers and citizens, for example.

Social science versus natural sciences and humanities

In order to distinguish the social sciences, we need to understand what the relationship is between two other distinct bodies of knowledge—the humanities and the natural sciences (including physical, earth, and life sciences). How is social science similar or different from the humanities and the natural sciences? Social science might be thought of as sitting on a spectrum between the humanities and the natural sciences. It is interested in many of the same questions as the humanities, but aspires to use many of the methods of the natural sciences to answer them. As the British political scientist Iain McLean has put it, 'social science is the scientific study of human beings . . . what distinguishes the social sciences from the humanities is not so much subject matter

13

as techniques . . . Humanities are (mostly) interested in the unique; social sciences are (mostly) interested in the general.'

Like the social sciences, humanities subjects such as philosophy, history, literature, theology, and art history are also interested in human beings and the social world. Unlike the social sciences, their focus is slightly different—on making sense of human experience, rather than explaining human behaviour, whether at an individual or group level. They examine human history, culture, and values, and try to interpret the ways people have understood and expressed themselves throughout history. The humanities generally do not necessarily seek generalization, but are interested in interpreting the unique perspectives and voices of particular people and cultures, as represented through, for example, literature, art, music, language, and stories. With few exceptions, most humanities scholars do not try to systematically identify patterns of behaviour that apply abstractly across different contexts, whether universally or given specific scope conditions.

Science seeks to create a systematic and organized body of knowledge, and it aims to do so based on scientific method—standardized techniques for building scientific knowledge. However, social science is distinct from natural science insofar as it examines the human-constructed world rather than the physical or natural world. This makes some of the objects of study more challenging to specify or measure. Key social scientific concepts like power, identity, and culture are less conducive to precise and consistent measurement than, say, gravity, time, and space. In the natural sciences, the researcher is also independent of the object of study, whereas in the social sciences, the researcher is a part of society—changing the scope for objectivity. Social science has its origins in attempting to emulate science's attempt to generate systematic knowledge based on evidence. Early social scientists found different ways to reconcile scientific ambition with the distinctive nature of the social world. Three contrasting examples can be found in the ideas of Auguste Comte, Max Weber, and Karl Marx.

Nineteenth-century French philosopher Auguste Comte was the first to coin the term 'social science'. He argued that society could be studied scientifically, just as scientists study the laws of nature. He claimed, 'the ultimate goal of society is to create a new science of humanity', and that thought about the 'social' had evolved across three stages, the theological, the metaphysical, and the positivist. Before Comte, philosophers and theologians from ancient Greece to Renaissance Italy had of course theorized about humanity, but what was novel in Comte's approach was seeking to combine theory and observation—verifying claims based on evidence. From Comte's so-called *positivist* perspective, set out in the 1848 *A General View of Positivism*, social science should focus only on that which can be observed and is measurable. Positivism is a term we will come back to later in this book, but broadly refers to the idea that the social world can be objectively understood, and studied using scientific methods.

Max Weber, a German sociologist, was among the first social scientists to question this positivist approach. He agreed that although society should be studied 'as a science', it required a distinctive *interpretive* approach to make sense of people's subjective social realities. He was essentially suggesting that to make sense of social action, we should ask people, 'what are you doing, and why?' His general theory was that people's actions are shaped by their cultural context (e.g. religion) because culture shapes meaning and motivation. But in order to study this, he suggested that social science needed what he called 'verstehen' (understanding), which he divided into observational understanding (watching what people do) and empathetic understanding (making sense of the meaning and motive attached to the act). His methodological challenge was to reveal people's emotions, beliefs, values, and interests, and show how they were shaped by culture. He used his verstehen approach to explore themes of social change; for example, in *The Protestant Ethic and the Spirit of Capitalism* (1905), he argued that Protestantism's values contributed to the formation of capitalism because it predisposed its subjects to actions and motives that enabled a new economic system to emerge and thrive.

Karl Marx, a German philosopher and economist, also believed it was possible to create a general theory of society, applicable across contexts. However, his approach, set out in *Das Kapital* (1867–94), can be considered a starting point for *critical theory* insofar as its goal was to unveil how power works in society and contributes to social transformation. Marx's theory was that society changes through class conflict. The nature of these class conflicts evolved with any given 'mode of production' (way of producing). In slavery, it was between slaves and owners; in feudalism, between peasants and landowners; in capitalism between workers and the owners of capital. In a capitalist mode of production, capitalists own the means of production (i.e. factories) and extract 'surplus value' from labour (the part of their productivity they can take in profits). This mode of production is the 'base' of society, and it also shapes the 'superstructure'—that is, culture (from religion to sport), which simply exists to appease and mollify the working classes. Eventually, Marx claimed the working classes would rise up in revolution and seize the means of production, ushering in a communist society.

All three of these foundational social science perspectives have had an enduring legacy. All of them aspired to create general social theories. Comte, Weber, and Marx all recognized the need to use evidence—gathered from archives, interviews, and data—to support theory. However, none of them fully resolved the question of what constitutes 'valid knowledge' in the social sciences. While aspiring to be systematic and rigorous, they fell short of what might be regarded as 'scientific method'—the process of objectively establishing facts through testing and experimentation. How would they know if they were wrong, when almost any piece of evidence might be selectively used to support their theories? For example, Weber and Marx make diverging claims about causality: for Weber, culture shapes the economic system; for Marx, the economic system shapes culture—but neither offered a means to establish who was right.

Writing in 1934 in *The Logic of Scientific Discovery*, Karl Popper, one of the 20th century's most influential philosophers of science, identified a way to address this. He rejected inductive research (inferring theory from observation), which had characterized social research up to that point, and instead argued in favour of deductive research (testing theory using observation). He argued that induction does not work because no number of positive observations can confirm a scientific theory, but a single counterexample can definitely show that the theory is false. He therefore further argued that falsification rather than verification is the basis for sound scientific method. The 'Falsification' Principle, for Popper, was central to scientific method: for a theory to be considered scientific, it must be possible to test it and conceivably prove it to be false. For example, the hypothesis that 'the world is flat' could notionally be falsified by observing that when you go around the world you end up back where you started. Popper's ideas implied a clear sequencing for 'good' social science: begin with a theory; posit a falsifiable hypothesis based on that theory; test that particular hypothesis based on systematic data collection; reject or do not reject that hypothesis; iterate and adapt the underlying theory.

In the last 90 years since Popper, scientific method has evolved considerably. But the idea of scientific method as a step-by-step process endures, and remains influential within the social sciences. There is broad consensus that it involves an iterative cycle covering the following steps: (a) formulate a question (that is clearly defined, testable, and measurable); (b) build a preliminary theory based on observation (usually relating to a cause-and-effect relationship, but which might be derived from induction); (c) form an explanatory hypothesis that is falsifiable (usually a prediction with an 'if...then' structure); (d) test the hypothesis through experimentation or data collection; (e) analyse the data and draw conclusions; (f) publish and share results; (g) iterate (repeat the cycle again).

The application of scientific method underpins the core of positivist social science research. For example, one of the most widely cited textbooks on social science methods is *Designing Social Inquiry* (1994), by Gary King, Robert Keohane, and Sidney Verba (henceforth KKV). This textbook argues that there is a single logic of inference that should characterize all social science research, whether quantitative or qualitative, which draws upon and adapts scientific method. Part of what is interesting is the adaptations that social scientists need to make to apply scientific method to the social world. For example, KKV highlight the particular need for social scientists to ensure that:

- concepts are 'concrete' (observable);

- theories are 'parsimonious' (explain a lot by a little);

- data includes 'variation' in the variables of interest (e.g. if you are interested in the impact of sex on educational attainment, you would need data that includes boys and girls, and different levels of educational attainment, as well as variation in other factors that might conceivably influence educational attainment).

For many positivist social scientists, adapting and emulating scientific method is the gold standard for 'good' social science. Herbert Simon, one of the most influential social scientists of the 20th century, claimed, 'The social sciences, I thought, needed the same kind of rigor and the same mathematical underpinnings that had made the "hard" sciences so brilliantly successful.' For others, the richness and potential of social science comes from embracing the challenges and complexities of the social world, rather than reducing them to simplified 'scientific' variables. Over time, positivist, interpretive, and critical approaches have all evolved and innovated, importing and exporting ideas from and to the humanities and sciences. The extent to which positivist, interpretive, and critical paradigms of social science dominate varies across different disciplines. Economics and psychology sit at the scientific end of the spectrum, anthropology closer to the humanities end of the spectrum, while disciplines like sociology and political science draw eclectically from both.

Today, contemporary social science is arguably a richer and more vibrant field because of the diversity and pluralism that characterize it, with researchers drawing from both the humanities and the sciences to come up with innovative answers to important social questions.

Chapter 2
Doing social science

What do social scientists actually do? The most important role of social scientists is research—systematic work undertaken to increase knowledge. Social research, though, is about more than just the gathering of information. While it can be a creative process, it needs to adhere to certain standards, to ensure that the findings can be regarded as accurate, or at least persuasive. These shared standards have emerged—and gradually evolve—within the community of social scientists. Social scientists hold one another accountable for maintaining those standards, including by reviewing one another's work before it can be published. Often, within university social science courses, students will take a research methods class. It will most likely cover data collection methods from interviews to archives. But what is also crucial but less commonly taught is the research design process—which is the focus of this chapter. How can you design an entire social science research project from start to finish?

Broadly speaking, social research has four main building blocks—questions, theory, methods, and empirical evidence. A *question* is something we want to know about the world, for which we do not already know the answer. It might begin with a 'why' (explaining a causal relationship) or 'how' (understanding something), or ask 'under what conditions' we observe something, or 'what factors' lead to a particular observed outcome. Usually there will be a central research question, but it might also be broken down into sub-questions. A *theory* is usually a systematic explanation for observed behaviour or outcomes. One starting point for finding a theory might be to go to the existing most relevant academic literature, see whether what other people have argued explains similar or related questions, and adapt that theory based on preliminary observations. *Methods* are the techniques and tools used to collect and analyse data. *Empirics* (or empirical evidence) relate to the findings derived from collecting data; for example, a statistical dataset on the experiences of older people living in care homes, or a case study about a particular country that adopted policies to increase girls' literacy.

With a few exceptions, good social science research will have all of these elements. Importantly, they will be in a coherent relationship to one another. A social scientist cannot simply cherry-pick their favourite topic, their favourite theory, and their favourite methods, and mash them all together. At least one element has to lead, and the others follow logically. Usually, the most important starting point will be the question. The theory will be chosen based on the question, the methods will be the best methods that are feasible given constraints like resources or the technical skills of the researchers, and the empirics will be the findings that follow from the application of the methods to an applied context, whether historical or contemporary. You will probably find all four of these elements in most good social science research articles or books, and in most social science research proposals—from undergraduate dissertations through to major research grant applications (Figure 1).

Different approaches to social science have divergent approaches to how these elements are most appropriately sequenced. Deductive research, which seeks to test theory, tends to have a question–theory–methods–empirics sequence. Inductive research, which seeks to build theory based on observation, tends to have a question–methods–empirics–theory sequence. In practice,

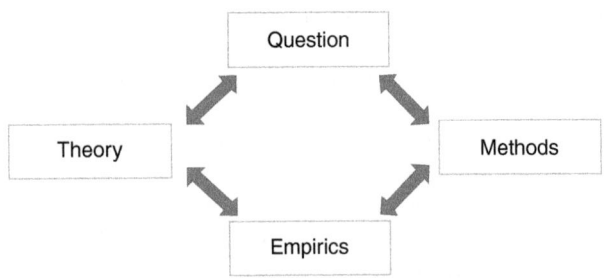

1. The four building blocks of social science research.

though, deduction and induction are often combined, as many researchers undertake preliminary research in order to build theories that can be tested. Deductive research follows a quantitative methods tradition, and inductive research a qualitative methods tradition; although either approach can in practice use quantitative or qualitative research, or a combination of both.

To unpack this further, there are broadly three different paradigms for social science research design: *positivist* (which builds on deduction), *interpretive* (which builds on induction), and *critical* (which often rejects objectivity altogether). They build upon the traditions that we touched upon in the previous chapter when discussing Comte, Weber, and Marx. Each of these paradigms has different purposes and different relative strengths and weaknesses. They all present trade-offs and choices, and there is no perfect way to undertake social research design. The three paradigms transcend disciplines but are sometimes found to a greater degree in particular disciplines. To some extent these paradigms comprise different communities of researcher, and doing 'good' social science means different things within each of those communities. There are debates about the extent to which the different paradigms can be combined or are inherently incompatible.

As Table 2 highlights, each paradigm has a different approach and purpose. They each have their own comparative advantage,

Table 2. Three paradigms of social research design

Research paradigm	Approach	Purpose
Positivist	Explanation (theory-driven)	Prediction/problem-solving
Interpretive	Understanding (data-driven)	Meaning/lived experience
Critical	Transformation (advocacy-driven)	Challenging power/knowledge

depending on what you want to study, how you want to study it, and what you are ultimately trying to achieve. Positivist approaches focus on explanation—why do we observe a particular behaviour or outcome? They are useful for solving practical problems or enabling prediction by identifying causal mechanisms. Interpretive approaches focus on understanding—how does a particular community or culture perceive a particular issue? They are useful to make sense of people's lived experiences. Critical approaches focus on transformation—they seek to make power visible. They are useful for challenging sources of oppression and marginalization. Below, I offer a simplified view of how each paradigm approaches social research design.

Positivist research design

Positivist research design continues to be the dominant paradigm, especially in North America. It is viewed as truly 'scientific' because of the extent to which it emulates scientific method more generally. Some disciplines such as economics and social psychology are almost exclusively based on a positivist paradigm, while others such as political science and sociology are more divided. There is, of course, no single research design process, and the stylized version in Figure 2 will inevitably need to be adapted to fit with

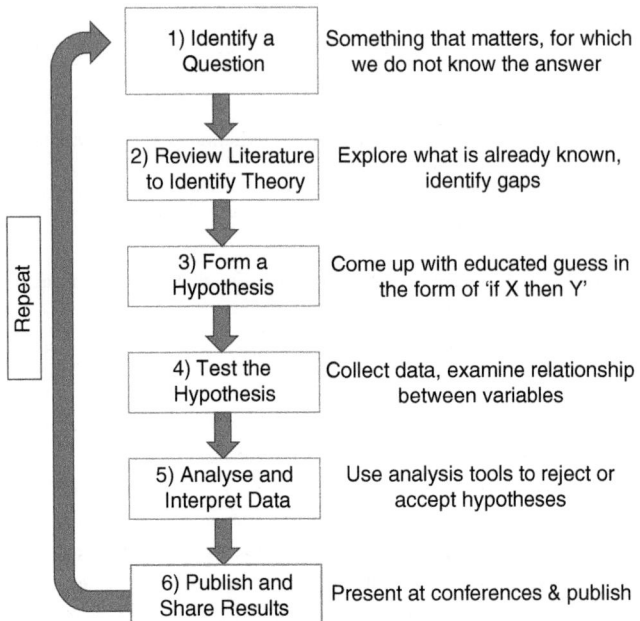

2. Positivist social research design process.

particular disciplinary norms. I outline the process sequentially, although it should also be noted that there may also be some back-and-forth between some stages—for example, it would be almost impossible to identify a question (stage 1) without first doing some exploratory reading (stage 2).

Positivist research begins with a clearly specified research question that relates to explaining variation in behaviour or outcomes. It is likely to take a form of 'why do people . . .', 'how does x influence y', or 'what factors explain . . .'; that is, examining the causal relationship between one or more variables. It might relate to individuals, households, companies, nation-states, or any other unit of analysis. Ideally, the question will be framed in the broadest possible way, even if you will ultimately answer it using evidence from specific places, time periods, or contexts.

This could be more than one question, although usually there will be a central question that might be logically subdivided. For example, the question 'what impact does contact between immigrants and receiving communities have on receiving community attitude to immigration?' could be logically split into sub-questions that progress from the general to the specific: (a) What explains variation in receiving community attitudes to immigrants? (b) What is the impact of contact on attitude formation? (c) How do different types of contact (e.g. economic or social) matter for attitude formation?

The question needs to be *answerable*—and for that the key elements in the question need to be sufficiently precise to be measurable (whether using quantitative or qualitative data). There also needs to be scope to observe *variation* in the key variables within the question. For example, if we are interested in the relationship between domestic violence (intimate partner violence) and recession, we need to ensure that we could potentially observe variation in these factors—looking at situations (across time or place) in which levels of domestic violence, economic circumstances, and any other factors that might affect domestic violence were at a range of levels. The answer to the question should also be *non-obvious*. It should be a question we do not know the answer to and should not lend itself simply to a yes/no answer. But we should want to know the answer because it is consequential; there is *something at stake*—ideally for both academic debate and for the real world. Usually, the question will be based on a so-called *puzzle*—a question for which no fully adequate answer can be found in the existing literature or theory.

To take an example from political science, Andrew Moravcsik wondered (in 2000), 'why did governments create international human rights regimes after the Second World War', given that this would—paradoxically—constrain their domestic sovereignty. To him, this was a puzzle because the existing literature appeared to offer an inadequate account. Within his discipline of international relations, he could identify two possible explanations from existing theory: a 'realist' explanation (that strong states would use them to impose norms of weak states) or an 'ideational' explanation (that states had been socialized into accepting the norms). Because he found these accounts unconvincing, he pursued a third alternative 'liberal' explanation (his hypothesis)—that powerful states might have committed to human rights institutions to deliberately constrain their own future leaders from undermining democratic governance.

Once you have formulated a question, you will need to immerse yourself in the existing literature. This may include synthesizing existing findings from the work of other social scientists. One of the defining features of academic social science is that it relates to—and builds upon—the work of a community of scholars, engaging with existing (shared) concepts and language. It may be that there is no literature or theory directly related to your particular question, but there may be a number of adjacent pockets of literature that offer relevant insights. Does any of the work highlight or hint at possible answers or causal mechanisms relevant to your central question? It's not necessarily about agreeing with, or replicating these; sometimes the most productive exploration comes from identifying work with which you intuitively disagree, or have grounds to believe may not provide a complete picture. A key part of this process is to identify 'gaps'. What is incomplete or even wrong? How might you build constructively upon what already exists? You might also complement your exploration of the existing literature with preliminary observations from the 'real world'. What have you seen—in the media, from conversations with people with direct lived experience of the issue, or from your general observations—that gives you a sense of what might explain your question.

To take an example from sociology, Lauren Rivera, who researches corporate behaviour, was interested in exploring the question of: 'what is the impact of culture on labour market hiring practices?' Her initial intuition—based on preliminary observation—was that elite consulting, law, and investment banking companies were not just hiring the most qualified people but the ones they regarded as a cultural 'fit'. In turning to the literature, she discovered two relevant existing bodies of work: one on labour market stratification showing that culture influences the sectors people work in; one suggesting that firms tend to select labour based on competence. But, she discovered a gap: 'systematic empirical research on the role of culture in hiring is virtually non-existent'. The combination of her own observation and her literature review enabled her to form her subsequent hypothesis: if applicants are a cultural fit with the culture of the firm, then they are more likely to get hired.

Based on your exploratory research, you will have a theory relating to your particular question—a sense of the relationship between variables and the mechanisms underlying that relationship. The next step is to put that in the form of a hypothesis. A hypothesis is simply a proposed explanation for something, or a cause-and-effect statement. It is essentially an 'educated guess', and is usually in the form of 'if X then Y'. Your hypothesis may follow convention (building in a complementary way on a dominant literature) or it may be unconventional (challenging received wisdom). Following what we learned about Karl Popper in the last chapter, hypotheses should also be falsifiable—it must be possible to find evidence that would lead us to reject the hypothesis. The convention within scientific methods is to assume that no relationship exists unless the evidence shows otherwise: we have a 'null hypothesis' (that no relationship exists between our variables of interest) and an 'alternative hypothesis' (that there is a relationship between the variables). If we find a relationship, we can reject the null hypothesis.

To take an example, Deni Mazrekaj, a professor working on the sociology of education, and his colleagues explore the impact of same-sex parenting on school outcomes. They review the literature and existing theory, much of which suggests a negative relationship (children with same-sex parents perform worse) because of three main mechanisms: (a) specialization (mothers and fathers play different roles), (b) kin selection theory (that people are more invested in their biological children), and (c) discrimination theory (the kids and their parents face prejudice). Based on a wider literature (with potentially relevant insights) and initial observations they suggest that the relationship is a positive one, and put forward a hypothesis for why this might be the case: *if* children have same-sex parents, *then* their school outcomes are likely to be better *because* of the selection effects arising from greater parental investment. Put simply, their educated guess is that, actually, same-sex parents are likely to be from higher socio-economic backgrounds and therefore invest more time, effort, and energy into parenting.

This is where we engage in confirmatory research to assess whether there is a relationship between our variables of interest. Crucially, positivist research will think about relationships in terms of a *dependent variable* (what we are trying to explain) and one or more *independent variables* (the factors we think explain or predict variation in the dependent variable). An example of a dependent variable might be people's income levels, and the main independent variable of interest might be education. In order to test the hypothesis that higher education levels predict higher income levels, we would also need a sense of the other 'control variables' that may influence income—such as occupation or household size.

In order to test our hypothesis, we would need to select relevant tools for collecting data relating to our variables of interest. Positivist data collection tools could be both quantitative or qualitative, and include surveys, direct observation, experiments, case studies, or archival research, for example. These methods would ideally provide data that measure a random sample of the population of interest. Coming back to our previous example, we might decide that we were interested in testing the hypothesis that higher education levels lead to higher income levels for individuals in cities in Bangladesh. We would not be able to claim that our findings were universally generalizable (to every place in the world), but we might select four cities that were representative of the country as a whole, and focus on slum areas in those cities. We would then seek to collect data from a small and randomly chosen sample of the population ('random sample') in each of those four urban slums. One way to test our hypothesis would be to simply survey this random sample, asking questions that gather data relating to all of our variables of interest. Another way would be to run an experiment—for example, delivering a higher or vocational education programme to part of the target population ('treatment group') but not to an otherwise similar group ('control group'), and observe what different outcomes arise, if any, over time.

Having collected the data, an important stage is the analysis of that data. With quantitative data, this may involve the application of statistical techniques, possibly including the use of software. In quantitative research, a lot of these techniques aim at establishing correlations (the extent to which two variables, X and Y, tend to change and move together), or—more challengingly—to infer a causal relationship between those variables. Correlations may be positive or negative. They may be weak or strong. Strong positive correlations include the relationship between the price of a good and the quantity of consumer demand, between rates of household gun ownership and national rates of homicide, or between climate change and the frequency of flooding and drought.

Importantly, correlation is not the same as causation. Causation is the idea that X causes Y—in other words, that Y would not have happened in the absence of X. Just because two variables are correlated, does not necessarily mean one caused the other. There are several reasons for this. The direction of the causal relationship could potentially be the other way around ('reverse causality'). For example, there is a positive correlation between health and income, but does better health lead to higher income (by increasing productivity), or does higher income lead to better health (by enabling people to spend more on a healthy lifestyle)? Alternatively, there may be a third 'confounding' variable—Z—influencing both X and Y ('omitted variable bias'). For example, there is a strong correlation between ice cream sales and shark attacks in the USA, but eating ice cream isn't going to lead to you being eaten by a shark! Here the omitted variable is, obviously, seasonal impact on beach attendance. With qualitative data, there are also a range of formal techniques for analysing data; these include qualitative software tools, as well as established techniques designed to explore whether Y would have taken place in the absence of X.

A key part of the research process is to share results, especially with the wider academic community. This process conventionally takes place in stages: share drafts for feedback, submit to scholarly journals, share with non-academic audiences. Social scientists will often present initial drafts of their research papers at specialist academic conferences or workshops. Many of the largest professional associations—such as the American Sociological Society or the American Political Science Association—are disciplinary, but a growing number of academic meetings are thematic and embrace interdisciplinarity, for example the International Studies Association or the Development Studies Association. Following feedback, social scientists will submit articles to peer reviewed journal articles, in which anywhere from two to five anonymous reviewers will be selected to read and evaluate the work. This can sometimes take several months, and a significant proportion of papers are rejected or require changes in order to be judged suitable for publication. Although this sounds onerous, it is regarded as an important way for the community of social scientists to uphold standards. On the other hand, as the Austrian philosopher Paul Feyerabend famously argued in his book *Against Method* (1975), the challenge of scientific standards being upheld by communities of like-minded academics is that they can sometimes be conservative. Beyond academic publication, many social scientists also share their work widely with non-academic audiences, including business, government, and civil society—sometimes translating their work into more accessible formats—policy briefs, blogs, opinion pieces, social media, or short films.

Positivist research design relies upon a process of iteration. Each output is a contribution to a broader stock of knowledge. Through each study new things will be learned, and theories refined. But through the research process, new questions and puzzles will arise. The researcher (or research team) that undertook the particular study may well identify subsequent questions for future research. Or others—people who read the published work and are inspired or disagree, or a new generation of graduate students—may pick up the thread, and decide that there is more work to be done within the same broad area. One of the exciting aspects of social science is precisely the possibility to feel part of something bigger than just yourself—to contribute to building a corpus of knowledge over time as part of a wider community of social scientists. Significant contributions become widely read and cited, and leave an important legacy through the generations of work they subsequently inspire.

Additional considerations

Three additional considerations are crucial for social research design. First, *validity* considerations. Positivist research design has to meet four validity criteria: (a) construct validity (key concepts have to be clearly specified and measurable); (b) internal validity (the extent to which what is measured accurately represents reality); (c) external validity (the extent to which findings are generalizable or can be applied to other specified contexts); (d) reliability (whether it is possible for the study to be replicated in a way that would lead someone else to derive the same or similar findings).

Second, *practical* considerations. Whenever a research process is designed it will face constraints. No research will be perfect because all researchers face trade-offs. The research design has to be possible to undertake given whatever limitations exist in terms of time, money, access to data or respondents, and the skills of the researcher and the research team. One thing social scientists get very used to is balancing what they would ideally like to do with managing a budget!

Third, *ethical* considerations. All research designs need to reflect deeply on the ethical dimensions of the particular project, and all academic social science research will need to undergo an ethics review process. A core principal of social science research is 'do no harm'—both during the research process and through the social impact of the research. A research ethics plan will need to outline any risks (to the researcher, to research subjects, and third parties) and how they can be mitigated; details of how informed consent will be obtained from all research participants; reflection on power and any vulnerabilities among research participants (e.g. especially if addressing sensitive themes or working with children); the benefits of the research; how data will be managed and stored to respect privacy; and whether any compensation will be paid to research participants for their time or other forms of reciprocity. The need to reflect on research ethics is not specific to positivist research design, and applies to all research involving human subjects.

Interpretive research design

It is important though to recognize that positivist research design is not the only approach to doing social science. Interpretive approaches are instead interested in understanding people's lived experience, on their own terms. They rely very much on inductive reasoning, and do not usually begin with concepts or well-defined theory prior to data collection. Such approaches tend to view social knowledge as culturally and historically contingent—in other words, there can be no generalization beyond context. Because interpretive research is trying to understand rather than explain, it does not frame research design in terms of independent and dependent variables, or explore correlations or causal relationships. Interpretive research is very common in anthropology, but also widely used in sociology, political science, geography, social archaeology, and interdisciplinary fields such as international development and education. It draws heavily on the humanities, and tends to use data derived from fieldwork or archival material.

To give an example, Bronislaw Malinowski was one of the earliest social anthropologists, writing *Argonauts of the Western Pacific* (1922). He undertook several extended periods of fieldwork over a five-year period in the Trobriand Islands in Melanesia. He did not have a defined theory before he first travelled to the islands, and he pioneered a method called participant observation—being part 'insider' and part 'outsider' within the community. He observed a phenomenon called the 'Kula ring'—of ceremonial gift exchange between the islands. Islanders with high social status would risk their lives making treacherous journeys on small boats to trade seemingly worthless trinkets made of shell (e.g. necklaces and armbands). To some this might have seemed just about trade, or puzzling that people would risk their lives moving these ornaments across choppy seas. But by understanding the Kula ring from the perspective of the communities, Malinowski theorized that the exchange process played an important role in political authority, the recognition of social status, and created reciprocal relationships between the islands. What might appear to Western eyes as a rather pointless economic transaction was fundamental to the politics of the islands.

Interpretive research is a diverse set of approaches, but it generally has a different sequencing from positivist research design. First, it begins with *identification of an area of study*. As above, this might well be a clearly defined research question, but it could also be a broad topic for initial exploration. Malinowski did not have a fully formed research question when he first visited the Trobriand Islands. Anthropologists sometimes find other ways to narrow down a topic in ways that do not prematurely impose structure on the community or topic. They work out what 'to follow'—for example, a particular people, objects (artefacts or technologies), practices, stories, or metaphors, but then remain open-minded about where that following will lead. The overall area of study might emerge from identifying under-researched themes in the literature or from preliminary observations about the world.

Second, it involves *fieldwork preparation*. Interpretive research does not necessarily have to involve fieldwork. Its methods can involve the use of text-based sources, including archival or historical material. But it frequently does involve some kind of fieldwork because it is usually focused on understanding people's lived experiences and so very often works directly with people, or with the artefacts (including books, letters, paintings) that they have created. The 'field' though does not have to be a far-away place, it might be found close to home, in a powerful institution, or in the virtual or online world, for example. Before data can be collected, there is therefore likely to be an important phase of relationship building with community gatekeepers, informants, partner organizations, in order to support safe and ethical access to communities and relevant artefacts.

Third, *data collection* is usually qualitative—although some interpretive researchers do occasionally use quantitative methods. It relies upon a combination of questioning and observation to develop a deep and granular understanding of a community. Often the starting point is to build 'thick description' or to gather unstructured textual data or transcripts (e.g. from documents or even digital sources) to be analysed. Anthropologists will often use ethnography, involving 'deep hanging out' with communities, to observe and understand them on their own terms. The initial aim is to faithfully reproduce people's lived experience, and document it in a form that can be analysed. In undertaking interviews, for example, interpretive researchers are likely to document more than just what someone actually says, but also non-verbal communication, informal interactions, and context.

Fourth, *data analysis*. One common way to think about the role of the interpretive researcher has often been as a 'translator' from one culture into another. In *The Interpretation of Cultures* (1973), American anthropologist Clifford Geertz discussed the need to see culture as working with unfamiliar texts written in unfamiliar languages about unfamiliar themes. Anthropologists frequently distinguish between the *emic* (from the research subject's perspective) and *etic* concepts (abstract categories from the researcher's perspective). An entire branch of interpretive research has borrowed from hermeneutic methods in the humanities in order to explore and debate ways of translating meaning across cultures. Hermeneutics is the theory and methodology of interpretation. It has been applied to social science to make sense of unspoken assumptions, habits, customs, and verbal and non-verbal communication. A hermeneutic approach to social science will aim to make sense of observations that go beyond just the content of what a research subject has said. For example, in order to study social class, a hermeneutic social scientist might observe and make notes on accent, body language, or examine the overall coherence of the narrative.

Fifth, *theorizing*. Following an inductive logic, interpretive research tends to theorize based on the insights of the data. Theory will often emerge by creating a conversation between the empirical findings and existing theory. How do the insights potentially change theory, or have relevance for long-standing theoretical debates? A so-called *grounded theory* approach involves collecting the data without theoretical preconceptions, organizing it into categories and concepts, and then relating it to the wider literature. Many interpretive researchers will shun aspirations of grand theory or generalization, and instead seek to develop 'heuristic' frameworks—conceptual simplifications of empirical findings. These will usually be provisional or only applicable to very specific contexts.

Sixth, *publish and share.* Interpretive researchers will publish their work in peer-reviewed academic journals, just as positivist researchers do. However, often they feel an additional sense of responsibility to share findings with communities that have contributed to the research. Given that interpretive research often involves working with people in a range of cultural contexts, it is often also important to take research findings back to those groups—either to receive feedback prior to publication or to ensure communities share in the benefits of what they have co-produced.

Critical research design

A third type of research design is critical approaches (Figure 3). In its most general sense, critical simply means making a rigorous judgement of something. In social science, however, it usually means something much more specific: it refers to approaches that problematize knowledge and expose structures of power. In contrast to positivist and interpretive approaches, critical research believes that 'all knowledge is for someone and for some purpose', and focuses primarily on making visible the power relations that underlie dominant ideas. What makes it distinctive from positivist and interpretive approaches is that it is more focused on critiquing existing knowledge than creating new knowledge. Its ultimate goal is social transformation—challenging institutions and ideas that contribute to oppression and exclusion. What marks critical approaches out as distinctive is their *epistemology*—their theory of knowledge understanding. A critical

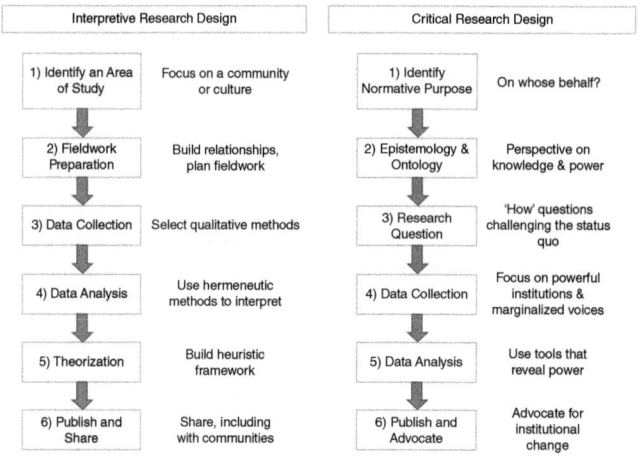

Interpretive Research Design		Critical Research Design	
1) Identify an Area of Study	Focus on a community or culture	1) Identify Normative Purpose	On whose behalf?
2) Fieldwork Preparation	Build relationships, plan fieldwork	2) Epistemology & Ontology	Perspective on knowledge & power
3) Data Collection	Select qualitative methods	3) Research Question	'How' questions challenging the status quo
4) Data Analysis	Use hermeneutic methods to interpret	4) Data Collection	Focus on powerful institutions & marginalized voices
5) Theorization	Build heuristic framework	5) Data Analysis	Use tools that reveal power
6) Publish and Share	Share, including with communities	6) Publish and Advocate	Advocate for institutional change

3. Simplified interpretive and critical research design processes.

epistemology rejects the idea that it is possible to objectively understand 'social reality', instead suggesting that claims to 'truth' are a reflection of power. Revealing these power structures still requires research, albeit of a different kind.

Michel Foucault's work offers an influential example of critical research. He was interested in the relationship between power and knowledge. He focused on what he called the 'pseudo-sciences'. For him, areas like criminology and psychology were not simply objective ways to look at social issues. They were a means to measure people's behaviour, establish norms of acceptable social behaviour, and enable institutions to observe, punish, and correct 'deviant' behaviour. His core concept was discourse—dominant ideas and practices. For Foucault there was no objective standpoint apart from the discourse. Discourse shapes all subject positions, including of the researcher and the research subject. As a social historian, his approach was to use archives to uncover the problematic and contingent history of dominant ideas and practices. For example, in his four-volume

The History of Sexuality (1976) he exposes the origins of dominant 20th-century ideas about human sexuality, and how they came to be used by institutions of the French state to control, normalize, and correct supposedly deviant practices.

Critical approaches cover a broad spectrum of methodological and theoretical perspectives—including Marxist, post-structuralist, post-colonial, anti-racist, and feminist scholarship. It is impossible to generalize across all of these approaches. However, it is important to highlight the ways in which they tend to differ from positivist and interpretive research design.

First, *normative purpose*. Much critical research starts from an explicitly normative position. It is concerned to address a particular form of social injustice, oppression, or exclusion. Its underlying goal is 'emancipation'—to liberate people from the oppression of dominant institutions and ideas. For Marxists, the focus is class-based oppression; for post-colonial researchers it is the legacies of Empire; for critical race theory it is racial oppression; for feminism it is gender-based oppression and misogyny; and for queer theory it is the oppression of sexual minorities. Critical approaches usually have their people—and the research is *for* them.

Second, *epistemology and ontology*. For critical researchers, theory and methodology are closely intertwined, and they are shaped by one's prior perspective on knowledge (epistemology) and being (ontology). Researchers will clearly elaborate their assumptions in these two areas. In terms of *epistemology*: how do you think about the ways we can know the world? A significant part of this will be about your own 'positionality' as a researcher in relation to the subject of the research. How do your own identity—in terms of race, class, gender, sexuality—and values influence the way you do research? Have you reflected on the ways in which your own historical context may create potential biases in relation to the research? In terms of *ontology*: how do you conceptualize the social actors you are studying? Are you interested in individuals, families, firms, nation-states? Can those social actors be thought of as if they were all rational self-interested actors, or are their identities shaped within their historical and cultural context. Do you believe that social actors are mainly influenced by material considerations like money (following Marx) or by discourse (following Foucault)?

Third, *research questions*. Critical approaches usually ask 'how' questions. One aspect of this is asking how it is possible that something that exists in the world today (an idea, institution, or practice) exists in the form that it does. Part of the disposition of a critical perspective is to approach the world with incredulity: to see contemporary manifestations of oppression and exclusion, and interrogate how they have come to be that way. It is to denaturalize the familiar—showing that things that seem widely accepted have emerged in a particular historical and cultural context, underpinned by power and interests. The underlying aim is that by destabilizing 'taken-for-granted' assumptions about the world, it becomes possible to imagine alternative future realities.

Another common angle for critical questions is to explore the strategies and tactics of resistance to oppressive institutions. How have marginalized or oppressed people mobilized to contest dominant institutions and with what degree of success? Sometimes, critical researchers co-design their research questions with affected people within the communities they are studying, based on the principle that the purpose of the research is ultimately to serve those communities. Examples of critical research questions include: 'how have legacies of empire shaped democracy in Africa?', 'how has racial capitalism shaped the pharmaceuticals industry in the United States?', 'how do indigenous people mobilize to challenge business investment in the Amazon rainforest?', and 'how do discourses of criminality shape immigration policy in Europe?' Often critical researchers may break a central question down into sub-questions to encompass a focus on both powerful institutions ('top-down') and the oppressed populations ('bottom-up'). For example, in *The Anti-Politics Machine* (1992), the anthropologist James Ferguson adopts this approach in using a Foucauldian methodology to critically examine the World Bank's development programmes in Southern Africa—ethnographically examining the perspective of both the World Bank and the affected communities.

Fourth, *data collection.* The choice of research methods will follow the epistemological and ontological assumptions that critical researchers hold. For example, because Foucault viewed all actors—including the researcher—as constituted through discourse, the methods he adopted focused on tracing the historical emergence of discourse over time. Because Marx viewed the world as shaped by social class, money, and materialism, Marxist methods often focus on revealing vested interests, and tracing the economic foundations of political institutions. Critical methods borrow heavily from the humanities and literary theory, and are diverse and creative, including archival research, interviews, ethnography, oral history, and dramatology (the use of drama to make research themes accessible). Sometimes, critical researchers may work collaboratively with practitioners or affected communities to collect data.

Fifth, *data analysis.* Critical approaches have a range of techniques for analysing qualitative data in ways that reveal power relations. Discourse analysis, for example, is used to analyse written or spoken text within its social context. Used effectively, it reveals how knowledge is embedded within particular patterns of power relations and identity construction. It does this by showing how particular forms of language and representation reflect underlying belief systems and justify, legitimate, and naturalize particular forms of behaviour. For example, in International Relations, discourse analysis has been used to show how particular forms of dominant knowledge held within US politics made actions such as the military invasion of Iraq and the

Cuban Missile Crisis possible. Much critical feminist research also used discourse analysis to reveal how underlying gendered assumptions enable the material oppression of women and girls. A vast range of other critical data analysis approaches exist—from semiotic analysis (following de Saussure), which looks at cultural signs and symbols, to deconstruction (following Derrida), which examines how binary concepts (e.g. natural/man-made) structure Western thought in hierarchical ways. It is also worth saying that some critical research is just straightforwardly empirical—providing factual evidence of power and interests.

Sixth, *publish and advocate*. Critical researchers also obviously publish academic work. But many also take especially seriously their underlying commitment to use their research for advocacy. Critical researchers often collaborate with NGOs on social campaigns or engage in activism in order to promote institutional change. For example, from campaigns to decolonize education to climate action and indigenous rights, critical research has often played a role.

Can the paradigms be complementary?

The three paradigms have divergent views on the process of social research. However, there are ways in which they might be considered partly complementary. For example, the *'theory-building'* approach of interpretive research is complementary to the *'theory-testing'* approach of positivist research. Interpretive research can inductively identify new questions, observations, and puzzles, which might be tested through positivist research design. Indeed, the idea of combining inductive and deductive approaches is increasingly common within research design. 'Abduction' is the name often given to approaches that either begin with induction and move on to deduction, or iterate back and forth between inductive and deductive approaches to develop and refine social theory.

Even where the approaches cannot be easily combined, they may still be able to work together in complementary ways, and also learn from one another. If part of the aim of social science research is to change society for the better, and address sources of inequality and injustice, then all three paradigms have a contribution to make. Despite their different starting points and divergences, they offer different pathways of influence.

Positivist research is often especially adept at influencing government and business 'from the inside' because it provides insight into the mechanisms through which changes in policy might influence behaviour or outcomes. Interpretive research can often help to shape political and social agendas by revealing under-researched or poorly understood themes. Critical research is often adept at influencing social change 'from the outside' by making hidden sources of power transparent in ways that are useful for advocacy campaigns or social movements. If our aim is to address global challenges affecting people and planet, there is an argument that each approach has a valuable role to play.

Chapter 3
Theories and concepts

Social science is full of theories—from those that explain inequality and poverty to racial exclusion and injustice. At its most basic level, a theory is simply an idea about the way the world works. Why do social scientists care so much about theory? Theory is used to understand (how things have come to be the way they are), explain (why we observe variation in outcomes and behaviours), and predict (what will happen if we do something). It is not intended to accurately represent the complexity of the 'real world'; it provides a simplification of reality. Theory is important for social science because it serves to organize and make sense of empirical observations (the data social scientists collect). Theory enables social scientists to build upon the work of others, to determine which data is relevant, and to move beyond description towards specific claims about how the world works.

Often the starting point for social science is to simply describe the world. However, description quickly gets boring. Raw facts don't interpret themselves, and if we just had facts, how would we even know which ones are relevant? For example, I may have a series of income measurements or high school test scores, but unless I have a basis on which to compare, assess, or judge them, they will be fairly meaningless. To make sense of them we need a 'lens' through which to interpret them or give them meaning. As one social scientist, Anol Bhattacherjee, put it, 'a collection of facts is not a theory, just as a pile of stones is not a house'.

But there are lots of different ways in which social scientists use theory. Within and across academic disciplines, it can be understood in different ways. Many anthropologists use it to identify a starting point for inductive ethnographic research. Many economists begin with a parsimonious (very simple) theory based upon assumptions and then deductively test them. You can't always combine and integrate every theory. Theory involves making choices about what is most important for you to be able to explain or understand. No one theory can explain everything—and the 'best' theory will depend on what we are interested in, whether we prioritize detail or simplicity, and whether understanding or explanation and prediction are most important to us.

The purpose of theory

There are many benefits of theory. It allows us to *make sense of facts*, and to see relationships between different observations. Data by itself does not have implications. The fact that I get an average of seven hours' sleep is itself banal and uninteresting. But once I understand that different age groups sleep different amounts and teenagers need to sleep later and perform better at school if they do, it becomes more interesting. Theory also enables us to engage meaningfully in *conversation across contexts*. Many social constructs—wealth, marital status, gender—are used in everyday discussion, but rarely defined. Theories assign a meaning to concepts, enabling them to be used more consistently. Relatedly, theory enables us to build a *cumulative body of knowledge*. Social scientists are not isolated individuals but part of a community. No one researcher will definitively resolve the questions they work on. They will make a contribution to knowledge, which others will build upon over time. In order to ensure that social science research can be built upon by others, it needs to be in a shared common language that is relevant across different contexts (places, historical periods, or communities). By abstracting from the particular to the general, theory enables social scientists to be in dialogue with one another, and to build upon one another's insights and findings. Finally, theory enables us to derive implications and make *recommendations*. Policy-makers and practitioners rarely want to know all of the details, and instead need simplified abstractions that can be used to change the world. Good theory—of all kinds—will support this, whether by highlighting causal relationships, supporting predictions, or disrupting dominant assumptions.

There are broadly four building blocks for most theory. Most theories, from most perspectives, will have each of these elements. First, *concepts*. Theory needs clear and measurable abstractions ('constructs'). In many cases these might be easy to measure—for example, income or weight—in other cases they may require a bit more creativity to formulate, whether because they are complex or highly abstract, for example mental health or ethnicity. Second, *relationships*. It needs propositions about how these concepts relate to one another. These could be causal relationships (X causes Y), or constitutive relationships (X socially constructs Y, i.e. X's social activity is necessary for Y to be what it is). An example of a causal relationship would be higher access to girls' education leads to higher economic growth and lower inequality. An example of a constitutive relationship would be how ideas relating to gender (perhaps what clothes boys and girls should wear) shape how people behave towards girls (the number of parents sending girls to school wearing pink clothes). Third, *mechanisms*. It needs a proposed logic for why it is that these relationships exist. For example, girls' access to education leads to higher economic growth because educated mothers make better decisions about nutrition and healthcare, have fewer children, and value their own children's education. Fourth, *conditions*. It needs clarity on the scope conditions under which the theory is applicable (when, where, and for whom?). Does the theory apply just to a particular community, a particular country, or the whole world?

That being said, there are at least two distinctive approaches to theory and theorization within the social sciences, which might be referred to as *explanatory* theory and *interpretive* theory.

Explanatory theory attempts to systematically explain social behaviour and outcomes. More formally, it can be defined as (based on Bhattacherjee's words) 'a set of concepts and propositions that interrelate to explain and predict behaviour under particular circumstances'. Explanatory theory is focused on finding the 'truth', identifying cause-and-effect relationships, explaining and predicting, and ensuring that theories build on one another. Sequentially, building an explanatory theory begins by identifying its key concepts—that is, properties of interest relating to people or outcomes. Some concepts, such as 'attitudes to immigration', 'violence', or 'levels of religiosity' may be more abstract than others, and the challenge is to specify these concepts as precisely as possible so that they are measurable. The researcher would then propose a relationship between these concepts in terms of variables: a dependent variable (effect) and independent variables (causes), clarifying any assumptions about when and there the theory might apply. An example of an explanatory theory is the law of supply and demand from economics—the theory that prices are determined by the relationship between supply and demand. The theory has a clear set of concepts (demand, supply, and price), and posits a set of relationships between these variables: if demand rises and supply remains constant, then prices will rise; if demand drops and supply remains constant, prices will fall.

Explanations can be *idiographic* or *nomothetic*. Idiographic explanations are those that explain a single situation or event in detail. Nomothetic explanations seek to explain a class of situations or events rather than a specific situation or event. They are meant to be generalizable across contexts. The former tend to be more detailed because they can relate only to a given situation; the latter tend to be less detailed because they have to be applicable across contexts. An example of an idiographic theory would be: the First World War happened because of the assassination of Archduke Franz Ferdinand in 1914. An example of a nomothetic theory also relating to war would be: wars tend to start because of changes in the distribution of power and alliance between nation-states. Most explanatory social scientists aspire to create nomothetic explanations.

So what is a 'good' explanatory theory? On what basis can we judge other people's explanatory theories? A list of elements might include testability—is it framed in a way that makes it falsifiable so that we can collect or analyse data that would, notionally, allow us to know if the theory was wrong? Consistency—is it logically coherent or does it contain internal contradictions between its propositions? Explanatory power—does the theory explain the data, and how much of the variance in the outcome of interest does it explain? Predictive power—can it explain the future, or does it work to accurately predict scenarios from the past? Parsimony—does it offer simplicity so as to enable it to be applicable across the broadest possible range of contexts? Finally, practical usefulness—is it possible for policy-makers, businesses, or practitioners to use the theory in ways that change and improve their decision-making? The last three of these will apply much less to idiosyncratic explanations, which is why nomothetic explanations are generally considered better.

In contrast to explanatory theory, interpretive theory attempts to understand the world from different perspectives. It can be defined as 'analytical frameworks to study and interpret meaning and motive'. Such approaches start from the assumption that there are multiple possible meanings and interpretations. Meaning is subjective (defined by individuals) and intersubjective (defined within groups). From this perspective, theory might be understood as analogous to maps. Theory is neither right nor wrong but its value depends on its purpose—a road map is different from a population map. Different theories reveal different things, and are useful depending on what you want to be able to see. Compared to explanatory theories, interpretive theories have particular strengths in being useful for understanding specific cultural contexts, or providing depth of analysis in areas of social complexity—such as motive, emotion, and aspiration.

To take an example of an interpretive theory, French sociologist Émile Durkheim's structural functionalist theory claimed that all social structures fulfil certain social functions, and in particular social institutions play a role in creating social order and long-term stability within a society. For example, the function of marriage is to raise children; the function of schools is to educate children and to create order and discipline; the function of funerals is to provide a mechanism that prevents the breakdown of social order by disposing of the dead. It is an interpretive theory because, although not easily falsifiable, it offers a lens through which observed social behaviour can be interpreted and understood. Interestingly, Durkheim's theory has been widely critiqued for underplaying the role of culture, neglecting conflicts over social institutions within a society, and struggling to make sense of how social institutions change over time. But it is still regarded as useful because it offers a particular lens, an insightful way of looking at social institutions.

So what is 'good' interpretive theory (Table 3)? How can we judge it? Originality—does it offer a new understanding of people and their behaviour that is not provided by other existing theories? Insight—does it make visible things that it would not otherwise be possible to see? Reflexivity—does it show an awareness of the positionality of the theorist relative to its subjects of interest? Community—does it have broad recognition from the wider community of similarly minded social scientists?

Table 3. Contrasting views on judging 'good' theory

Explanatory Theory	Interpretive Theory
Falsifiability	Originality compared to alternatives
Explanatory & predictive power	Insight that would not otherwise be possible
Consistency in terms of internal logic	Reflexive awareness
Parsimony	Recognition by scholarly community
Practical usefulness	Potential for societal reform

It may not be right or wrong—or even falsifiable—but it will be more or less persuasive relative to alternative interpretive theories. Societal reform—does it have the potential to bring progressive social change, whether by directly influencing policy and practice, or indirectly by disrupting conventional understanding and shaping public debate?

Grand theories

Theories exist at different levels of abstraction. The highest level of abstraction in social science is often referred to as 'grand theory'. It relates to theories that try to provide a general explanation of human behaviour or society. They seek to explain large-scale relationships and answer fundamental questions such as why societies form and why they change. They are often then used as starting points to guide theory-building or theory-testing at an applied level. Grand theories often serve as what American philosopher of science Thomas Kuhn called 'paradigms'—shared standards for research within a particular area, evolving through new revolutions in thought. Here, I outline four examples of influential—and frequently debated—grand theories within the social sciences, each with a distinctive epistemology (i.e. understanding of what counts as knowledge). Each one has its own particular perspective on one of the most fundamental questions in social science: the relationship between structure (social arrangements that emerge from and determine human action) and agency (the decision-making and behaviour of people).

The first grand theory I will address, *rational choice*, begins from the premise that individuals maximize their own interests based on cost–benefit analysis. This theory assumes that individuals are self-interested, and have clearly ranked preferences in relation to a given choice, and maximize what is often referred to as their 'utility'—their overall satisfaction or happiness. The approach is enormously valuable because it enables observed behaviour to be theoretically interpreted. For example, the law of demand and supply outlined above is only possible to interpret based on an assumption that a rational person will be interested in maximizing the quantity of a particular good for a given price, or minimizing price for a particular quantity of a good. Similarly, in criminology, Deterrence Theory suggests that the higher the sanction (prison term or fine) for a given offence, the lower the likelihood of the crime being committed. This observed empirical relationship only makes sense based on an assumption of the criminal as rational actor—weighing up the benefits, probability of being arrested, and likely punishment if caught.

Rational choice theory has even been applied to areas assumed to be subject to emotion or culture—such as marriage altruism or civil war. The approach is commonly criticized for being too simplistic a view of human decision-making. However, this is not an entirely fair criticism: rational choice theory does not claim to accurately represent how people actually make choices. Rather, its value is that it helps formulate clear and falsifiable hypotheses, and then enables empirical observations to be interpreted in ways that would not be possible if we viewed people as making random or impulsive choices. Rational choice theory is commonly used in economics, political science, and sociology.

In addition to examining individual decision-making it can also be applied to a variety of forms of social interaction. For example, it can be used to interpret the observed behaviour of corporate actors, such as firms, nation-states, or organizations based on an assumption that these corporate entities behave like individuals (methodological individualism). It can also be used to understand strategic interaction between people. Game theory, for example, offers a simplified way to understand the interaction between two or more individuals (or other actors) based on the assumption that they are rational actors who will therefore respond to the behaviour of the other in rational and predictable ways. It has been used for everything from modelling the interaction of the United States and the Soviet Union during the Cold War to businesses' consumer pricing strategies. Social exchange theory has emerged within sociology to similarly understand how relationships between two people are created through a process of cost–benefit analysis on both sides—examining everything from online social interactions to employer–employee relations. An example of social exchange theory is being asked on a date, and deciding to go on the date if the pros outweigh the cons.

Second, *social constructionism* views people's identities as constituted (shaped) by their interactions with others. And, in turn, these identities determine people's interests and hence their behaviour. In contrast to rational choice, then, people are not assumed to have predetermined identities and interests, but rather these are the result of their social interactions. For social constructionists—sometimes referred to as constructivists in political science, for example—the aim of theory is to shed light on the process through which ideas, identity, and interests are socially constructed. Pierre Bourdieu and Anthony Giddens are two of the foremost contributors to social constructionism. For Bourdieu, people acquire 'cultural capital'—their habits, skills, and dispositions—throughout their lives. These come to be embodied in something called 'habitus'—socialized norms that guide thought and behaviour. For Bourdieu, while habits shape people's behaviour, they still have some degree of agency to choose and, in turn, to shape habits. Bourdieu applied these ideas to understand the transmission of cultural practices in mountain communities in Algeria. Giddens formalized social constructionism through the concept of 'structuration'—the notion of an iterative relationship between structure and agency. Structure (ideas, norms, institutions) shape individuals' identities, but individuals in turn have the possibility to stand back, reflect, and shape the structure around them. These ideas have been applied to understand everything from children's socialization within high school education to the ways in which intergovernmental norms emerge and influence state behaviour.

Third, *Marxism(s)*, which we have already touched upon, offer a range of approaches that understand society—and social change—through the lens of social class conflict. Within the capitalist mode of production there is a division between owners of capital and labour; the former exploit the latter by extracting the value of some of what they produce ('surplus value'). These relationships ('the base') in turn explain particular cultures ('superstructures') that support the legitimization and maintenance of these exploitative relationships. In contemporary research, neo-Marxism takes on a variety of forms. One tradition is highly empirical—largely shunning theory and instead focusing on revealing *'qui bono?'* (who benefits) from dominant social institutions and practices. This tradition aims to expose vested interests and the role of the capitalist economy in perpetuating injustice (for example, the work of Antonio Negri and Michael Hardt). Another tradition is much more theoretical, and for example focuses on the way in which particular forms of superstructure play a role in upholding the base (following the work of Antonio Gramsci). Still other approaches seek to theorize the structural relationship between capitalism and politics, whether nationally or internationally. For example, Dependency Theory looks at the world as divided between 'core' and 'periphery' based on nation-states' position in relation to particular factors of production—the core holding capital, and the periphery mainly having land and labour. Its central claim is that the economic development of the core and the underdevelopment of the periphery are 'two sides of the same coin'. Put simply, the rich get rich by impoverishing the poor.

Fourth, *post-structuralism(s)* view society as shaped by dominant forms of knowledge that are inextricably linked to power. As the name suggested, they emerge from a critique of so-called 'structuralism' which tried to identify underlying universal structures across all human societies. For example, structuralist Claude Lévi-Strauss argued that all the main myths across all societies were reducible to a few common underlying structures, while Ferdinand de Saussure argued that all languages are reducible to a common underlying structure. Post-structuralism rejects this perspective. Instead, it views the social world and culture as if a 'text', but that this text can only be understood in the context of the system of knowledge and power within which it was produced and the system of knowledge and power within which it is being interpreted and analysed. For post-structuralists such as Michel Foucault, the world is constituted through discourse (shared language and practices), and this discourse shapes all subject positions—including those of the researcher and the research subject. There is no standpoint apart from within the discourse.

For most post-structuralists, power operates as what Foucault called 'productive power', whereby discourse shapes and entrenches hierarchies, power asymmetries, and forms of exclusion and oppression. Two key related ideas are 'governmentality', the way in which people are governed through controlling how they think about the world, and 'biopolitics', the way in which bodies and populations are controlled and managed. Post-structuralist theories have generally been applied to social science by drawing upon the work of a handful of mainly French social theorists, including Foucault, Jacques Derrida, and Gilles Deleuze. Within contemporary social science, such theories have been applied to explore ways in which dominant structures of knowledge and categorization shape the world—for example, the division of the world into 'North/South' or 'developed' and 'underdeveloped', the labelling and exclusion of 'migrants' and 'refugees', or the way some human lives are valued and others are not.

Middle-range theories

In practice, most social scientists aim to build, test, or adapt middle-range theory, which seeks explanations that are specific to very particular social phenomena. They can be used as a starting point to guide the formulation of research questions. Examples of middle-range theories include: 'contact theory', which posits that the more groups from different backgrounds interact, the better they get along; 'reference theory', which suggests that people take the standards of people close to them in making judgements about themselves or others; and 'conflict theory', which implies that the inequitable distribution of resources, power, and status between groups may lead to conflict. Middle-range theories may or may not have a clear relationship to a particular grand theory. In contrast to grand theories, their more specific focus may make them useful for providing practically relevant insights or supporting particular interventions.

Many middle-range theories have particular disciplinary origins but are often influential beyond that discipline. In economics, *Principal–Agent Theory* posits that in any managerial or organizational relationship there is likely to be delegation from a 'principal' to an 'agent'. The interests of the principal (e.g. the company's owners) are not perfectly aligned with those of the agent (e.g. its managers), and cannot efficiently oversee all aspects of the agent's behaviour. Information asymmetries (the agent knowing more) or conflicts of interest often result in 'agency slack', meaning that the agent will often act in ways that do not align perfectly with the interests of the principal. The theory has been applied to a range of contexts from the role of sports agents to brokers in financial markets, and the delegation of authority from nation-states to international organizations.

Another widely influential middle-range theory from economics is *Prospect Theory*, which explains how people make choices when faced with risk and uncertainty. It shows how people do not assess 'loss' and 'gain' equally, as rational choice theory might assume. Instead people are often 'loss averse'—for instance, the negative feelings they would get from losing £50 in a game of cards would be greater than the enjoyment they would get from winning the same amount or more. The theory has been used across a variety of applied areas; in political science it has been used to look at why political leaders with a strong democratic mandate often avoid important but risky policy choices. International relations uses it to understand risk assessment in wartime decision-making by governments.

In psychology, the *Hawthorne effect* suggests that employees may increase their productivity if they are observed in their environment, even if nothing else changes in that environment. The theory emerged from experiments that looked at how being watched (and other changes in working conditions) affected employee motivation. The theory has been applied widely, not just in psychology, but across management studies, for example, to consider ways in which particular types of feedback can improve productivity. Similarly, Herzberg's *Motivation Theory* suggests that employees are not only motivated by wage and salary levels, but by other motivational factors such as recognition, professional development, and workplace satisfaction. These experimental findings have been applied widely to reconsider incentive structures beyond pay rises or bonuses—influencing how social science thinks about interests, motives, and incentives, from politics to household chores. Kohlberg's *Theory of Moral*

Development meanwhile identifies three stages through which people develop the capacity to act and think ethically: pre-conventional (an understanding that actions have consequences, and so the ability to understand the costs and benefits of compliance with rules), conventional (an ability to accept sources of authority and recognize standards of behaviour), and post-conventional (an ability to develop and reflect upon one's own values and standards). The theory has been influential in thinking about business practices in management studies, child development in education studies, and moral action in political science, for example.

In sociology, a variety of middle-range theories have emerged, for example, to explain discrimination—whether in relation to race, gender, or other identity categories, sometimes grouped into *Discrimination Theory*. To take a few examples. Attribution Theory suggests that in-groups tend to categorize out-groups and assign to them derogatory connotations, which often explain the in-group's negative outcomes by bad luck, and the out-group's positive outcomes by good luck. Scapegoat Theory suggests that in-groups (let's say US citizens) often blame out-groups (migrant workers from Mexico) for perceived harms to the in-group, such as unemployment. Conflict Theory sees discrimination as the consequence of competition over scarce resources. Social Dominance Theory suggests that better-off in-groups tend to create discriminatory discourses—such as nationalism and xenophobia—to legitimize inequality and sustain their superior socio-economic status. These different theories—and many others—have often been combined or integrated with theories from other disciplines, to generate hypotheses in relation to particular applied interdisciplinary contexts, such as to examine how and why receiving societies sometimes discriminate against immigration. It is not that any one of them provides the full picture, but that they can be useful for identifying particular variables of interest that will differ in their degree of relevance.

In political science, *Collective Action Theory* has become one of the most influential theories. It focuses on the ways in which individuals will often act in ways that are sub-optimal for the group. American political scientist Mancur Olson developed the ideas with a focus on so-called 'public goods'—things like street lighting, which have the properties of 'non-excludability' (once provided everyone benefits regardless of who pays) and 'non-rivalry (one person's enjoyment does not diminish the enjoyment of someone else). Other examples of public good include national defence, roads, fire services, and clean air. The argument is that unless there is an institutional provider, these goods will be under-provided relative to what people would choose if they consulted and acted together. The theory has been developed drawing upon game theory, and based on a rational choice model. It has been widely applied to address a range of real-world contexts. For example, Elinor Ostrom and Oliver Williamson won the Nobel Prize in Economic Sciences in 2009 for outlining ways in which collective action failure affects areas such as ecological preservation, drawing upon the related idea of the 'tragedy of the commons'—that short-term self-interest leads people to inadequately care for shared resources—such as rivers, oceans, and forests.

Another example of an influential middle-range theory from political science is *Democratic Peace Theory*, which suggests that democratic states will not go to war with one another. Building on ideas from German philosopher Immanuel Kant's *Perpetual Peace* (1795), political scientists such as Michael Doyle elaborated the idea that democracies do not go to war with one another. The observed empirical relationship seems to hold well for inter-state conflict between liberal democratic states, although there has been debate about the precise causal mechanisms, with some researchers highlighting the role of democratic norms restraining the use of force and others suggesting it comes down to democratic political structures such as the role of the legislature and the judiciary in raising the barriers to acts of war. The theory, though influential, has also been criticized for failing to account for liberal democratic states' tendency to use force against non-democracies or to become involved in internal armed conflicts.

The range of middle-range theories across the social sciences is vast, and these few examples are far from exhaustive. But they hopefully illustrate just some of the exciting theories that have emerged from different disciplines, and the implications they have subsequently had beyond their disciplines and for real-world challenges.

Key concepts

Concepts are not theories. But they are one of the essential building blocks for theories. They specify, define, and enable measurement of the most important ideas within a theory. Traditionally, specific disciplines prioritize particular concepts within their research agendas. Disciplines use many concepts, but most disciplines are associated with a central concept. These central concepts give their disciplines a main focus, but are—in almost every case—not used and applied across the social sciences. Here, I outline five key social science concepts, each emerging from a particular discipline, that are essential for interdisciplinary social science.

Political science's defining concept is arguably '*power*'—the ability of one person (or organization or country) to get another to do something they would not otherwise do. Power is not an attribute that is possessed; it is relational—it is an actor A's ability to get an actor B to do something they would not otherwise do. It is also a highly contested concept, with different perspectives on what it means as a concept, informed by different epistemologies (what counts as knowledge) and ontologies (from whose standpoint we look at the world). American political scientists Michael Barnett and Raymond Duvall outline four types of power

Table 4. Typology of the concept of power

	Direct	**Diffuse**
Constraining	Compulsory	Institutional
Constitutive	Structural	Productive

based on a 2 × 2 taxonomy. Power can be conceptually distinguished along two axes. It can be 'direct' (going directly from actor A to B) or 'diffuse' (going from A to B via some intervening mechanism). It can also be 'constraining' (using rational incentives, whether carrots or sticks) or 'constitutive' (shaping how people see their identities and the world). From this 2 × 2 taxonomy, they derive four types of power (illustrated in Table 4). Compulsory power relates, for example, to the use of guns or money to change someone's behaviour. Institutional power relates to how actors influence institutions to deliberately create rules that control what others can do. Structural power relates, for example, to how people persuade or create narratives to influence how other people see themselves and their interests (following neo-Marxist ideas of how culture is used to support capitalism). Productive power relates to how discourse (in the Foucauldian sense) shapes everyone's subject position in ways that often entrench inequality. Power is notoriously difficult to research, but is central to social science.

Geography's defining concept is *'space'*—the relational positioning of objects—crucially, geographical space, focusing on the relationship of objects to one another. At its most simple level, this might be about measuring 'what is where' in terms of distance and position. However, space is about more than measuring relative positionality on a map. It is also about the meaning that people ascribe to those relationships, as well as understanding how they came to be the way they are, and their social implications. For example, political geographers are interested in how power interacts with space in ways that influence identities and create policies that regulate space in areas from immigration to the management of urban slums. Geographers use a variety of techniques to understand spatial relationships, from topography to critical visual methods and discourse analysis. Ideas of space have been adopted by social scientists more broadly to think about themes from culture to geopolitics.

One of law's core concepts is *'norms'*—appropriate behaviours for a particular social actor. Types of norms include rules, customs, mores, and taboos. Much of scholarly law is interested in interpreting what the law is and what it means in particular contexts (jurisprudence). However, socio-legal studies more broadly are also interested in how norms emerge and change (norms as dependent variable), and their social effects, including for people's behaviour (norms as independent variable). As with 'power' above, norms can also be studied either as 'constraining' (creating carrots and sticks for particular types of behaviour) or 'constitutive' (shaping people's identities and worldviews). A range of disciplines and interdisciplinary approaches to social science adopt norms as a central variable, exploring themes such as state compliance with international law, violence-related codes of honour in street gangs, and the emergence of school playground behaviour.

One of the key concepts emerging from sociology is *'identity'*—the qualities that are used to characterize people. Some of these categories include gender, race, religion, nationality, sexual orientation, and social class. Social identity relates to who we believe ourselves and others to be. It is both personal (how you see yourself) and social (how others see you). Identity can be understood differently from different epistemological perspectives. For positivists, it is a variable that can be measured. For many interpretivist researchers, identity—and the meaning ascribed to it—is socially constructed. The way identity is conceptualized by social scientists has significant implications for how they analyse the world, and for the insights they provide. For example, in both economics and political science, 'ethnicity' has been viewed as a central variable in explaining civil war. Some 'positivist' researchers have shown how different types of ethnic fragmentation underlie civil conflict while many 'interpretivist' researchers have instead focused on either the social construction of ethnicity or its manipulation by political elites.

Anthropology focuses on *'culture'*—the ways in which shared ideas and practices influence behaviour. Culture encompasses people's shared cognitive worlds—their values, beliefs, traditions—as well as the social institutions that underpin them. Culture encompasses social structures that are transmitted through social learning, and social scientists tend to explore how culture changes, and how it affects behaviour—including through the socialization or acculturation of people. Anthropologists, as well as cultural sociologists, and cultural psychologists, for example, do not only study 'remote' or 'different' cultures, but also often try to look critically at their own cultures, or particular social institutions. Many engage in 'studying up'—examining elite institutions within their own society. American-German anthropologist Franz Boas spoke about *Kulturbrille*, or 'culture glasses' to refer to the 'lenses' through which a person sees their own culture—often unable to look at it critically, or apart from their own culture.

These concepts are just illustrative of some of the most important concepts in the social sciences. Although each one has its primary origins within a particular discipline, they have all become important across the social sciences and within interdisciplinary research. In each case, they are also highly contested concepts, with significant debates on how they should be epistemologically understood and studied. Each one is also methodologically challenging to use, defying easy measurement. While these and other concepts therefore represent the 'raw material' of social science, they leave social scientists with lots of room for creativity in how they are adapted and applied to different contexts.

Chapter 4
Methods and methodologies

A crucial part of social science research is collecting and analysing data. This might be primary data (collected by the researchers themselves) or secondary data (collected previously by someone else). An important distinction often found in social science is between 'methodology' and 'methods'. *Methodology* refers to the rationale and justification for the selection of methods to solve a particular research problem. What is the philosophical basis for the social scientist's approach? Are they doing positivist, interpretive, or critical research? What is the underlying epistemology? What is the balance between qualitative and quantitative research methods, and why? Are there particular ethical considerations relating to the research? *Methods* refer to the particular tools and techniques used to collect and analyse data—for example, surveys, interviews, or experiments. In Chapter 2, we unpacked some of the considerations relating to methodology; in this chapter, we delve into the most common social science methods—what are they, when might you use them, and how can you analyse the resulting data? It is important to be aware of what good standards of practice look like in relation to a range of methods, not only to be able to apply them, but also to understand and critically evaluate how they are used by social scientists. By understanding the methods used in social science research, you can form a judgement on the validity of the findings, claims, and insights of a piece of research.

Generally, social science research methods are divided into quantitative and qualitative methods, based on whether they mainly use numerical or non-numerical data. Some disciplines such as economics are highly quantitative, and others such as anthropology are highly qualitative. However, it is important to be aware that there is not always a sharp divide between these approaches. Many social scientists use 'mixed' methods, combining the relative strengths of quantitative and qualitative research. When students are training as social scientists, it is also important to learn both quantitative and qualitative methods, in order to be able to interpret and assess research that comes from different perspectives, and to be able to collaborate meaningfully with researchers who specialize in different research methods.

Qualitative methods

Qualitative methods relate to the collection and analysis of data that is usually non-numerical. They are especially useful for understanding how people experience the world. What meaning do events or actions have for a particular group of people? For example, what does marriage mean within a particular community? How is anxiety experienced within different cultures? How does a particular religious group relate to sexual minorities? How do newly arrived immigrants navigate employment markets?

In general, what are the pros and cons of qualitative research, relative to quantitative research? Qualitative research has lots of *advantages*. Exploration—it is especially useful when there is no existing theory on a topic and initial exploratory research is needed. Depth—it is useful for in-depth analysis of a particular historical or cultural context. Voice—it can ensure that the perspective and experiences of otherwise marginalized communities are respected and included. Adaptability—the approach can evolve with the research, being flexible in response to new observations and insights. It also has *disadvantages* and limitations (relative to quantitative research). Generalizability—it is usually not generalizable beyond the particular context. Comparison—some qualitative researchers do undertake comparative research, but it may be challenging to collect comparable data based on replicable methods from different contexts. Subjectivity—the researcher's own perspective is often central to qualitative research, and a different researcher could have a different interpretation of the same context.

These pros and cons are generalizations, and it is important to be aware that there are many different approaches to qualitative research. These pros and cons apply most obviously to qualitative researchers who are focused on meaning-making within a particular community (interpretive approaches). However, it is worth being aware that some qualitative researchers have tried to develop methods that enable structured comparison and the identification of patterns across contexts (positivist approaches).

Ethnography is a term that derives from two ancient Greek words, 'ethnos' (people or folk) and 'graphein' (writing or study). Put simply, it focuses on studying people in their cultural context. It aims to learn about and describe communities' customs, habits, traditions, and practices. It traditionally involves an extended period of fieldwork to observe communities over time. Strictly speaking, ethnography is not just one method, but involves a range of techniques to systematically record observations about a particular community. The most important of these is participant observation, which is a technique for observing communities from within. The researcher aims to be part 'insider' and part 'outsider'—getting to know the community on its own terms through active participation while still retaining a degree of critical distance. Because it involves spending significant unstructured time with research subjects, participant observation has been referred to as 'deep hanging out' by Clifford Geertz. This might involve spending time with particular individuals, families, community organizations, businesses, or sports teams, for example.

The hallmark of ethnography is the attempt to understand communities on their own terms. It does not assume that those communities can be understood by applying externally derived or 'Western' concepts and theories. In order to think about this, it often distinguishes between 'etic' ideas (those that are external to the community) and 'emic' ideas (those that are internal to the community). Even common ways to categorize the social world—such as 'law', 'economy', 'politics'—are usually avoided in ethnography, as a particular community may have quite different ideas of how to categorize their own practices. For example, sometimes what looks like an economic activity—like cattle ownership—may have a particular cultural meaning, with religious or spiritual connotations. Or sometimes what looks like a religious practice—such as witchcraft—may actually have a role in legitimizing political authority.

Classic ethnography, pioneered by early anthropologists, often focused on long periods of fieldwork in faraway communities. For example, British anthropologist E. E. Evans-Pritchard's book *The Nuer* (1940) was based on many months spent with the Nuer community in the south of Sudan. He pioneered ethnography as a means to try to understand the community on its own terms, seeing the role of the ethnographer as a 'neutral' role, with a cultural relativist perspective, avoiding making judgements based on his Western values. Since then critical ethnography has taken a different approach. Berkeley-based anthropologist Laura Nader developed the idea of 'studying-up' to suggest that ethnography should not only focus on communities 'out there' but also examine power and systems of governance. Following Nader, ethnography has been applied to look at, for example, the politics of the European Union, including through examining the cultural practices of civil servants within the European Commission in Brussels. This has opened up avenues for ethnography to be used across a range of disciplines; political science and international relations researchers, for example, now sometimes use ethnography to examine political practice. In addition to classic and critical ethnography, a whole series of innovative approaches to ethnography have emerged—'rapid' ethnography (involving short periods of fieldwork), 'online' ethnography (studying internet-based communities), and 'auto' ethnography (reflecting on the lived experience of the authors themselves).

Interviews focus on asking questions through one-to-one conversations. They are typically divided into structured, semi-structured, and unstructured. Structured interviews usually involve a survey questionnaire in which all respondents are asked identical questions. Semi-structured interviews involve drafting a flexible interview guide that may be specific to the respondent. Unstructured interviews are free-flowing conversations. Semi-structured interviews are perhaps the most common qualitative research method, and involve some preparation, but also the flexibility to actively listen and adapt. They are often thought of as 'guided conversations'. Interviews often complement other methods—they can be a standalone method, or combined with, for example, ethnographic or archival methods. They may also be used at the start of a project to shape research questions.

There are three main purposes to qualitative interviews. First, background information—they can be used at an exploratory stage of the research. Second, perspective—they can be used to understand how respondents interpret their experiences of the world around them. Third, evidence—they can be used to elicit information relating to events in the past and their sequencing, rather as though creating an archive. The key to designing in-depth interview questions is that they should be relatively open-ended questions, as opposed to 'leading questions' that presuppose a particular response.

The interview process can be divided up into stages. To start with, contact respondents—it is necessary to get access to respondents, build trust and rapport, and ensure that respondents understand the aims and purpose of the research and give their informed consent to participate, whether identifiably or anonymously. Then conduct the interview—ensure that an interview guide has been prepared, and that you actively listen throughout the interview, in order to improvise where needed. Finally follow up—consider sharing any direct quotations with respondents for their approval and share final outputs with respondents, depending on what was agreed.

An important question with interviewing is: how do you know who to interview? Unlike quantitative research, qualitative interviews usually do not use 'sampling'; instead researchers try to identify the people or organizations that have relevant perspectives, and ensure that a diverse spread of different perspectives is explored. For example, if I want to understand the impact of a particular refugee policy, I will often aim to speak to refugees, members of the host community, governments, NGOs, and United Nations staff. How do you know when you have interviewed enough people? There is no right answer or formula for calculating this. A good rule of thumb is when you have reached 'saturation'—you find that you are not getting access to new material and the same themes and stories are repeating. Once interviews have been conducted, there are different approaches to analysing interview material. These include 'thematic analysis', in which recurring themes are 'coded' in order to identify recurring patterns; and 'discourse analysis', in which the focus is on the language used, its connotations, and what it reveals about underlying power structures.

Examples of influential research based on semi-structured interviews include Paul Richards's (1996) *Fighting for the Rain Forest* in which he examined the recruitment of militias in Sierra Leone's civil war, including the motivations of young men for joining armed groups, and Paul Willis's (1977) *Learning to Labour*, in which he followed 12 working-class boys' experiences of a school in Birmingham, speaking several times to the children, as well as teachers and parents. In addition to focusing on people's own lived experiences, an important aspect of interviewing is 'elite interviews', in which policy-makers, politicians, or business leaders, for instance, are the focus. For example, in her book *The Trouble with the Congo* (2010), Severine Autesserre interviewed UN peacekeepers working in the Democratic Republic of Congo, including senior leaders, as well as ordinary people affected by peacekeeping operations.

Focus group discussions (FGDs) involve generating discussion among a selected group of people. FGDs are used to explore people's thoughts, feelings, and opinions relating to a particular topic, or sometimes to generate consensus around events and facts. They involve several elements: a topic, a moderator, a group of people (typically 6–10), and a venue (which may be in-person or online). Preparing for and planning an FGD involves different stages: a welcome—in which an overview of the topic is provided and any ground rules (e.g. on recording and use of material) are made clear; engagement questions—these are general and open-ended questions relating to the topic; exploratory questions—specific questions that elicit the material that is of greatest relevance to the researcher; and exit questions—asking participants if there is anything else they would like to highlight that has not already been mentioned.

FGDs involve challenges that need to be carefully managed by the moderator. Power dynamics are especially important to consider in relation to both who is in the room and the dynamics within the room. In many communities there may be 'gatekeepers' who restrict access to particular voices or try to influence the composition of the group. Similarly, within the group, some voices may be more influential than others. Both of these concerns are especially important relating to, for example, gender, age, and ethnicity. How can you ensure that an appropriately diverse set of voices is included? For example, when I have conducted FGDs with communities in refugee camps in East Africa, there has sometimes been a cultural expectation that FGDs will comprise mainly older, male community leaders, potentially marginalizing the perspectives of women and young people. There are also challenges to managing the behavioural dynamics of any particular group. There are risks of acquiescence bias (that people tend to want to agree positively with others) and social desirability bias (that people tend to want to look good and virtue-signal in front of others), to name but two. A skilled moderator will be aware of these and try to find ways to mitigate them by, for example, highlighting that 'all perspectives are equally valid', 'it is OK to disagree', and 'there are no right or wrong answers'.

Despite the challenges, FGDs are especially useful for researchers interested in what is called 'inter-subjectivity'—the perspectives that are shared by people, as opposed to those held 'subjectively' by individuals. How is it that groups think about issues or have developed commonsense conceptions about the world within a given cultural context? Put simply, it gives an insight into what psychologist Irving Janis called 'group-think'. Political scientists, for example, have used FGDs to understand political opinions and attitudes, and their formation.

Process tracing is a method for trying to understand cause-and-effect relationships between events in the past. So far, most of the qualitative methods we have discussed are used to understand people's perspectives, thoughts, feelings, and beliefs. But qualitative methods can also sometimes be used to understand causal relationships within particular case studies (how an independent variable, X, affects a dependent variable, Y, within a particular context)—for example, how democracy affects peace within the context of Sub-Saharan African politics. Alexander George and Andrew Bennett pioneered process tracing as 'an analytical tool for deriving causal inferences from a temporal set of events'. Their aim was the greater systematization of qualitative methods, documenting the mechanisms that connect actions and outcomes.

Process tracing focuses on the within-case analysis of cause-and-effect relationships. It is especially widely used to examine the impact of policy on a particular outcome. To what extent can the observed outcome of better educational attainment in maths be causally attributed to a policy to change the curriculum? It is also widely used in political science and international relations to examine historical cause-and-effect relationships; for example, to answer questions such as 'what influence did the Suez Canal Crisis have on British decolonization?'

The process generally involves the following steps: identify a causal hypothesis ('X caused Y'); specify and describe the independent variable (cause) and dependent variable (effect); theorize the causal mechanisms (i.e. the arrows linking cause and effect); analyse observable manifestations of those mechanisms by dividing the activities into component parts and identifying 'traces' (mechanistic evidence) that connect X and Y (such as money in a bank account), demonstrating that in the absence of those mechanisms, the observed outcome would not otherwise have been possible; and consider using comparative methods to explore the general applicability of these mechanisms across a number of other cases.

One of the most widely cited examples of process tracing is international relations scholar Nina Tannenwald's 'nuclear taboo' (1999), which shows how the American public's horrified reaction to the use of nuclear weapons in Japan at end of the Second World War led to the emergence of a norm of non-use of nuclear weapons by the US government during military crisis. In order to apply process tracing, she follows the steps outlined above by identifying her hypothesized causal explanation (that norms matter), discussing alternative possible explanations (that states are simply deterred by fear of other states using them), clearly describing the independent variable (that a public reaction occurred and that it was widespread, leading to a taboo) and the dependent variable (that the USA has shown nuclear restraint at key moments), identifying the causal mechanisms connecting independent and dependent variables (i.e. that elite policy-makers shame proponents of use to become silenced), finding sources of historical evidence from archival research that evidence these mechanisms, and exploring the applicability across a series of cases (she traces her proposed mechanism across four key historical moments).

One of the key analytical features of process tracing is what is called 'counterfactual analysis'—determining that an outcome could not have taken place in the absence of a particular action. It relates to internal validity—the degree of confidence that X caused Y within the particular context. But this in turn raises questions about the standard of evidence required for a valid counterfactual. Political scientist David Collier highlights four different standards of proof (or tests) for counterfactual analysis. First, *straw-in-the-wind* (plausibility)—X is neither a necessary nor sufficient condition for Y, but there is evidence of plausible impact (e.g. the presence of a gun and of a dead person). Second, the *hoop test* (necessary but not sufficient)—X is a necessary condition for Y and so the explanation should stay in contention (e.g. a gun is found that matches the bullet found to have killed the dead person). Third, *smoking gun* (sufficient but not necessary)—X is a sufficient but not a necessary condition for Y (e.g. a person is found holding a gun that has just been fired and matches the bullets that killed the dead person). Fourth, *doubly decisive* (necessary, sufficient, and exhaustive)—X is a necessary and sufficient condition for Y, and no other explanations are plausible (e.g. a person is found holding a gun with a unique set of bullets matching the one that killed the dead person, and nobody else could have entered the room because it was locked). Unsurprisingly, Collier likens process tracing to the work of Sherlock Holmes.

Process tracing is often a complement to *archival research*, which involves extracting information from historical documents, records, and other sources (such as material objects—known as 'artefacts'). Archival research can draw upon personal, national, or organizational records, libraries, or special collections. Archival research is perhaps the most important research method of history and is also widely used in other disciplines, including anthropology and international relations. There is significant debate (as I mentioned above) about whether history should be most appropriately viewed as a humanities or social science discipline. It depends partly on how it is studied (and, of course, how we view the boundaries between the social sciences and the humanities). But there are certainly social scientific ways to study the past, especially when researchers are interested in using process tracing and counterfactual analysis to identify cause-and-effect relationships or in examining patterns of behaviour across contexts.

Quantitative methods

Quantitative methods relate to the collection and analysis of data that is usually numerical. They use statistics to investigate and interpret numeric variation in the social world—across time, place, and people. Variables (things that vary) might include income, people's well-being, educational attainment, immigration, and political attitudes. And quantitative methods offer a range of ways to describe patterns, reveal correlations, and test causal relationships between variables. For example, social science has used quantitative methods to show that happiness increases with income up until a threshold, then shows no further increase as income grows.

In contrast to qualitative methods, quantitative methods are especially effective for testing the generalizability of a theory beyond a particular case study. They allow comparison across contexts because the same or similar data are usually collected from different groups. They are especially useful for assessing cause-and-effect relationships. They also aspire to use methods that can be repeated by another researcher (i.e. they are 'replicable'). For example, if a psychologist designs an experiment to test whether children who read more develop greater empathy, it should be possible for another researcher to follow the same methods, and come up with similar findings. The downside of quantitative methods compared to qualitative methods is that they tend to work with 'averages' and so struggle to account for unique experiences. They are also at quite a high level of abstraction, and so may miss important details in people's experiences. They also tend to use externally derived categories and measurements to organize the world, and so may misunderstand or ignore communities' own ways of thinking about the social world.

There are often high barriers to entry to advanced quantitative methods, which require the mastery of mathematical or computational techniques. However, the basic principles are straightforward, and can be made accessible to all with a degree of simplification. In this section I will cover ways of collecting data and ways of analysing data. One way of simplifying quantitative methods for data collection is American sociologist Matthew Salganik's three approaches: observing behaviour, asking questions, and doing experiments.

Observing behaviour involves analysing things that are already happening and can be measured, without the need to interact directly with research subjects. Salganik's understanding of quantitative 'observation' is therefore very different from what qualitative researchers mean by observation. In particular, he is focused on using existing datasets. These might be government census data, opinion polls, house price data, or corporate data on consumer behaviour, for example. They do not require an intervention, and are widely used, even in journalism. Indeed, many datasets are now available online and can be easily downloaded to Excel or quantitative software programs for analysis.

In order to generate original insights, social scientists may combine datasets. For example, if you wanted to examine the role of university education in internal migration patterns from rural to urban areas in the UK, you might combine datasets from publicly available sources such as the British Social Attitudes Survey (which includes, for example, people's home relocation choices, educational qualifications, and income levels), with Government Land Registry Data on house prices. Or, if you wanted to examine the role of ethnic diversity in civil war, you could combine data from the Uppsala Conflict Data Program with the University of Maryland's Minorities at Risk dataset. Drawing upon—and sometimes merging—existing datasets provides researchers with a low-cost and ethically less challenging (compared to collecting your own data) way to explore patterns within the social world.

Asking questions offers a means to generate new data, when existing datasets are inadequate for answering a particular research question. The main way to do this is by conducting surveys. Designing a survey enables the researcher to decide what to measure and how to measure it. This requires a questionnaire—a set of closed questions for gathering comparable and measurable information from respondents. Questions will usually provide a limited range of possible responses, which should be mutually exclusive (not overlap) and exhaustive (cover all possible responses). They may, for example, be 'yes/no' questions or offer a set of ordered or unordered options, possibly on a scale. It is important that statements are clear so that they will be interpreted in the same way by all respondents, even across different populations of interest.

A key feature of surveys is 'sampling', which involves trying to ensure that the people who are interviewed represent a representative subset of the larger population of interest. If you are interested in the perspectives of students on sport at your university, you are not going to be able to interview all 20,000 students, and if you were to go and speak only to students going into the sports centre, you'd only get the perspective of those already doing sport and miss the ones that don't do sport. So you need to find a way to ensure that the subset you do speak to give you insights that represent the entire student population.

How can you do that? The most obvious method is *'random sampling'*—ensuring that everyone within the population has an equal likelihood of being chosen. To do this you would need a (contactable) list of the entire population and then simply randomly select the ones to be interviewed. The required sample size will depend on factors such as the overall population size and how much variance there is in the population, but as a rule of thumb is likely to be more than 100.

If your population of interest divides into groups who live in different areas, for example in different halls of residence within the university, or in different districts of the city, and you want to achieve greater representation across these units, you might use an approach called *'cluster sampling'*, which divides the population into smaller groups (usually geographical or institutional) which are 'weighted' within the sample according to their relative size within the overall population. This is especially important if you think people may give different answers to questions based on where they live. Respondents can then be randomly sampled from within these clusters. The role of cluster sampling is to ensure that you get greater representation across these units.

Alternatively, if you are especially interested in exploring patterns among a particular subgroup of the population (usually based on identity)—for instance, female students or ethnic minorities—you might use *'stratified sampling'*, which divides the population into homogeneous (similar) 'strata', and then randomly sampling within each stratum. This enables the strata to be analysed both independently and as part of the overall sample.

Crucially, sampling requires a sample frame—basically, a list of the overall population with identifier information and contact details. Common examples include electoral registers, telephone directories, or lists held by NGOs relating to their target populations. If you do not have access to a sample frame, you may sometimes be able to construct one. In my research with refugees, the United Nations Refugee Agency was sometimes able to provide a sample frame based on refugees' registration data. When this was unavailable or outdated, our team needed to put together our own sample frames. We did this by using a combination of satellite images and community mapping, working with residents to draw maps of the villages and residential blocks within the refugee camps. We were able to use these to undertake cluster sampling, and thereby achieve a representative sample of the overall population, across the different parts of the camps.

Doing experiments involves seeing what difference an 'intervention' makes to outcomes. It provides a means to test a hypothesis under controlled conditions. For example, one might wish to test whether allocating 'cash assistance' rather than 'food assistance' leads to better outcomes for victims of a humanitarian crisis. A social experiment relies upon several conditions. First, it requires being able to fully manipulate the independent variable. In the above example, this relies upon being able to fully influence the amount and type of assistance that the victims of crisis receive. Second, it relies upon being able to assign people to a particular 'treatment group' or 'control group'. In the example above, this requires being able to choose to assign (or randomly assign) some people—with otherwise similar characteristics—to a group that receives cash assistance, a group that receives food assistance, and possibly also a (control) group that receives no assistance at all. Third, it relies upon being able to create controlled conditions so that variation in other potential influences on the dependent variable are kept to a minimum (or at least known).

Experiments are especially useful in social science because—unlike most other methods—they offer the promise of what is called 'causal inference', being able to attribute an outcome 'Y' to a particular cause 'X'. This is especially the case when people with similar characteristics are randomly assigned to the treatment and control groups. For this reason, there has been a proliferation of studies across the social sciences in approaches that use experimental methods. Psychology has traditionally used experimental methods, but over the last two decades economics and political science, in particular, have used what are called Randomized Control Trials (RCTs) as a form of experiment, on which people with similar characteristics are randomly assigned to treatment and control groups, under controlled conditions. The RCT method—long used in medical experiments—has grown especially important in behavioural science, as well as in public policy experimentation, in order to assess what difference particular policy interventions actually make. RCTs have been used to test everything from microfinance, female literacy, efforts to combat school absenteeism, and vocational training programmes across the global South within development economics to the effect of positive social media campaigns on attitudes to immigration in political science.

The great strength of experimental methods, such as RCTs, is that they give an insight into causal mechanisms and often lead directly to policy recommendations on how to change people's behaviour or attitudes in areas such as education, health, or climate change. However, they also pose challenges. These include the ethical issues relating to 'experimenting on' people and communities, the difficulty of assigning people randomly to a 'control' group and depriving them of access to the services the trial is testing, and the context-specific nature of the experiment making generalization difficult.

Once data have been collected, there are three broad approaches to quantitative data analysis. First, *descriptive statistics*, which organize, summarize, and present data. This might involve presenting frequencies, percentages, or averages in graphs, tables, or infographics. Descriptive statistics are often useful for communicating trends accessibly and accurately to diverse audiences. They are frequently found in newspapers and magazines, as well as academic publications. For example, a pie chart can show the breakdown of a particular population by age group or ethnicity. A line graph can reveal trends such as changing levels of economic growth in a country over time. Descriptive statistics can be a useful starting point for reviewing data and identifying patterns in the data. They can be contrasted with 'inferential statistics', which explore relationships between variables.

Second, *correlations* explore the associations between variables. They can be described as strong or weak, and may be positive or negative. For example, in most societies, there is a strong, positive relationship between education and income. There is a strong negative relationship between smoking and life expectancy. Social scientists use a method called 'regression' analysis to reveal associations between variables. Regression analysis examines the influence of one or more independent variables on a dependent variable, using specialist computer software. At its simplest, social scientists will look at relationships between two variables (single linear regression), and the software will draw a 'line of best fit' to identify the general trend, and then provide information about the relationship—the direction of the effect, whether it is positive or negative, whether it is statistically significant (that we can be confident that there is a high probability the observed relationship is not the result of chance), and the size of the effect. In order to do this, a series of assumptions about the data need to be made: that it was collected based on a representative sample, that the relationship cannot be explained by a missing third variable, and that the relationship is linear (a straight line rather than a curve).

Regression can also be used to explore complex relationships between a number of variables. This is called 'multivariate regression analysis'. This will involve looking at the impact of a number of independent variables on a dependent variable, and assessing the relative significance and effect of each variable. This approach requires an additional assumption that the independent variables do not influence one another. An example of a multivariate regression analysis might be to examine the role of several independent variables (income, age, proximity of residency to a city centre, ethnic background, household composition, bicycle ownership) on a dependent variable (car ownership). The results might give us a range of information—for example, that income, home location, and household composition have a statistically significant relationship with car ownership; more specific information about effect size (e.g. some studies have suggested that a 1 per cent increase in income is associated with 2.5 per cent increase in car ownership); and whether any independent variables have a relationship to one another (e.g. that the effect of urban proximity is greater for certain types of household composition such as young couples than others such as young families).

Third, *causal inference* is the ultimate aspiration of much quantitative research. As social scientists are acutely aware, correlation is not the same as causality (or in the commonly used Latin phrase, *post hoc ergo propter hoc*—afterwards therefore because of—is a logical fallacy). As already noted, there are several reasons for this, including omitted variable bias (we may not have included all the relevant factors in our regression); reverse causality (the correlation does not tell us about the sequencing of the variables); sampling error (the sample may not be representative of the population of interest); measurement error (what we are interested in may be hard to measure). In order to make a valid causal inference, three conditions have to hold: (1) there must be a correlation between the variables; (2) the independent variable must precede the dependent variable; (3)

the correlation cannot be explained by some other (confounding) variable that is related to both. Social scientists aspiring to achieve causal inference need to design methods that meet these conditions. Experimental methods and impact evaluations (such as RCTs) that examine cause-and-effect relationships are widely used because they are capable of meeting these conditions.

Mixed methods

Qualitative and quantitative methods are often usefully combined within what is called 'mixed methods research'. This approach is useful because qualitative and quantitative approaches each have their own strengths and weaknesses. Qualitative methods are especially useful for theory-building and quantitative methods for theory-testing. The former often prioritize an inductive approach and the latter a deductive approach. The former enables in-depth understanding of communities in particular contexts and the latter enables exploration of the generalizability of theoretical propositions. A mixed methods approach has several advantages, including creating a rich dataset that combines numbers and stories, balancing depth and generalizability, and incorporating the perspectives and voices of research subjects. A recurring challenge for social science is how to effectively integrate such approaches—whether within collection, analysis, or discussion of findings.

Three broad approaches to mixed methods work stand out: *sequential design* (e.g. using qualitative research to inform quantitative design); *embedded design* (e.g. collecting both together within an experiment); *convergent design* (comparing qualitative and quantitative results to support validation). In my own interdisciplinary research on refugees, I frequently use a mixed methods approach, usually based on sequential design. I often begin with in-depth qualitative research in order to build a deep understanding of communities, develop relationships of trust, and undertake sufficient preliminary research in order to ensure meaningful quantitative research design. Sometimes after undertaking quantitative data collection, whether based on surveys or experimental methods, unexplained puzzles will remain or the causal mechanisms underlying correlations will remain opaque. Here, follow-up qualitative research, including based on in-depth interviews or focus groups, can help shed light on possible causal mechanisms. In one aspect of our quantitative research in refugee camps, for example, we found a correlation between nationality and participation in certain types of economic activity (agriculture or commerce). We discovered that Somali refugees were disproportionately more likely to engage in commerce but less likely to engage in agriculture than other nationalities. Understanding the reasons for this required a return to qualitative methods.

Chapter 5
How social science can change the world

Many people study social science because they want to make a difference. They believe that by better understanding and explaining society, culture, and the economy, it becomes possible to influence behaviour, policy, and practice. Often researchers and students will select their areas of study based not simply on intellectual curiosity, but because of a deeply held and values-based commitment to progressive social transformation. This might be race equality, children's rights, or environmental justice. Nearly all social scientists acknowledge these underlying motivations, and try to be open about what motivates their work. A particular challenge for social scientists, though, is to ensure that their own beliefs do not shape or invalidate their social scientific research. While methodological and theoretical choices may be shaped by underlying beliefs, a key part of social science is that researchers can justify their methodological choices, and have a commitment to 'truth', whether or not the findings ultimately align with the researcher's beliefs.

In the past, many social scientists were concerned to ensure their research was 'objective'. Any societal impact would be an unintended outcome of the research. And while dissemination (sharing research findings) would often happen after the research had been published, it was not necessarily something that would be planned in advance of the research. Today, the 'impact agenda' is central to social science. In order to get research funding, whether from governments or private foundations, social scientists usually need to be able to plan and demonstrate how their research will lead to impact—who are the research-users and how will the research shape decision-making across government, business, and society? The aim of this chapter is to explain and illustrate how social science research can have impact on the 'real world'.

Designing research for impact

'Impact' relates to the contribution of research to society and the economy. It exists at different levels: individuals, organizations, and countries. And it can take place via different mechanisms. The Economic and Social Research Council (ESRC) identifies three types of mechanism: (1) *instrumental*—directly influencing policy, practice, or behaviour; (2) *conceptual*—changing understanding and reframing debates; (3) *capacity-building*—developing technical and professional skills across society. Instrumental impact might involve sharing research findings with a government in ways that lead them to change policy or legislation, in an area such as gambling or immigration. Conceptual impact might occur when an idea such as 'resilience' transforms humanitarian policy and practice. Capacity-building might take place if a researcher translates findings into training for practitioners, in an area such as educational practice in schools.

It is now common practice for impact to be planned at the outset of a research project. Impact is about more than doing research and then sharing the findings as an afterthought. Many research funding bodies, including those that fund PhD students, require that proposals outline clearly how the research will translate into positive impact on society and the economy. Universities will often showcase impact case studies, sometimes structured in ways that outline the societal challenge, the research that was undertaken, and evidence of the resulting social impact. Prizes such as the ESRC's 'Celebrating Impact Awards' have been created to support a culture of impact across the social sciences. Impact often involves what is sometimes called 'knowledge exchange'—two-way exchange between researchers and research-users. Knowledge exchange activities might include seminars, workshops, placements, or direct collaboration at particular stages of the research process. Sometimes 'non-academic' organizations or groups of people may also be included in the research as co-investigators.

Some researchers have been critical of the impact agenda. They have suggested, for example, that it is important for researchers to be able to pursue 'policy irrelevant' research, given how rapidly relevance can change. Basic research or critical research, with no obvious application, can also be valuable as a means to advance social science. For example, some of the more important work in social science has been largely theoretical, and emerged through researchers having the autonomy to reflect deeply on social systems. Big thinkers within social science such as Marx, Bourdieu, and Jürgen Habermas have had profound real-world impact—but not necessarily on the basis of planned knowledge exchange with business or government. Many critical social scientists are cautious about the idea of 'problem-solving' social science, seeing part of the value of social science in its ability to stand apart from, and retain independence from, powerful institutions such as government and business. So it is important to recognize that 'impact' is embraced to different degrees by social scientists.

There are three broad pathways through which social science may have impact.

First, *describing and highlighting a neglected social issue*, sometimes through powerful critique. For example, Emla Fitzsimons and Praveetha Patalay's research on adolescent mental health led Public Health England to expand its mental well-being strategy from those who access mental health services to all children. Meanwhile, Raj Chetty and colleagues at the Harvard Opportunities Lab have revealed the racial disparities in social mobility in the USA in ways that have shaped the policies of government, universities, and non-profits across the country. Research might also offer a way to reframe an issue, such as by offering a new way of measuring something. For example, Kevin Bales's global study on the dimensions of modern slavery led to the adoption of his Global Slavery Index as the baseline against which the United Nations measures its Sustainable Development Goals progress towards ending slavery by 2030.

Second, *proposing solutions by revealing causal mechanisms.* Identifying correlation or causality can offer insights into the kinds of policy levers that might be effective in shaping social outcomes. A significant proportion of social science is focused on identifying the 'correlates' (the factors associated with something) of either harmful social practices—such as war, human rights violations, gambling disorder, domestic violence, depression, child abuse, divorce, or knife crime—or of positive behaviours and processes such as democratization, charitable giving, paying taxes, or compliance with international law. For example, researchers have explored the predictors of homelessness, examining factors related to lack of human capital, social exclusion, and mental health. The findings from this type of research have often been the basis of evidence-based policy-making by governments and other organizations.

Third, *evaluating or testing solutions*, including by using randomized control trials (RCTs), experiments, or impact evaluation methods. For example, Travis Baseler and colleagues used an RCT to study whether receiving community attitudes to refugees could be positively influenced by including members of the receiving community in aid programmes for refugees. The RCT conducted in Kampala, Uganda, showed that cash grants given to both refugees and the host community within the same programmes increase support for admitting more refugees and for letting them work and integrate locally. The findings have influenced World Bank and the UN Refugee Agency in their thinking on assistance programmes that target both refugees and the host community.

Below, I outline some examples of major societal challenges, for which responses have been improved as a result of interdisciplinary social science research—poverty, transport, malaria, child literacy, and policing.

Poverty

Around the world, 650 million people live in extreme poverty (on less than $2.15 per day). Sabina Alkire founded the Oxford Poverty and Human Development Initiative (OPHI) at the University of Oxford. The general assumption had always been that income poverty is a good measure of people's deprivation. But Alkire's work suggested that it is not just income that shapes deprivation, but also factors such as malnutrition and poor sanitation. With colleagues, she created the multidimensional poverty index, with three dimensions: health, education, and living standards, covering 10 measures, and seeking to understand the relationships between them. The index has subsequently been adopted by governments around the world, including Mexico, Bhutan, the Philippines, and Colombia, while influencing the thinking of organizations such as the United Nations Development Program (UNDP). Governments that have adopted the measure, such as Colombia, have reported how adopting the index has enabled them to change policies in ways that have taken millions of people out of poverty.

Abhijit Banerjee and Esther Duflo co-founded the Abdul Lateef Jameel Poverty Action Lab (J-PAL) at MIT. Their starting observation was that for too long development policies had been mainly based on instinct or ideology, rather than evidence of what actually works. They set out to use RCTs and experimental methods to test development interventions, building a network of hundreds of researchers around the world and carrying out more than 1,600 randomized evaluations. They have been able to test interventions such as cash transfer policies, microfinance schemes, the role of government regulation, initiatives to tackle corruption, and ways to increase girls' access to primary education, for example. One of their general findings has been that the world's poorest people are not irrational in their choices, but that they lack information and often have incorrect expectations—for example, in relation to the returns to education, leading them to make sub-optimal choices. They have collaborated with governments, NGOs, and the UN, reaching 600 million people through their programmes. As a result, they and their long-time colleague Michael Kremer became the first development economists to win the Nobel Prize for Economics in 2019.

Transport

Many social scientists are interested in understanding, and finding ways to influence, people's behaviour in relation to climate change. An important element of this relates to transport, which (excluding aviation) makes up around 25 per cent of greenhouse gas emissions, and is the leading source of emissions for many countries. Consequently, a growing number of researchers focus on explaining people's transport behaviour. What explains people's modes of transport and their routes? One aspect of this relates to people's choices to move away from car dependency towards alternative forms of transport such as cycling. Private car ownership not only contributes to climate change, but also to congestion, air pollution, and road-traffic death. In Copenhagen and Amsterdam around 40 per cent of commuter journeys are by bicycle, compared to fewer than 1 per cent of commuter journeys in the USA. Yet, social scientists have observed that policies can make a difference. Between 1990 and 2008 Washington, DC, tripled its number of cyclists by introducing a cycling network and rolling out a bike-sharing scheme.

The field of transport studies has explored some of the factors that lead to people shifting from cars to bikes and other forms of active travel. For example, infrastructure, bicycle access, bicycle equipment, costs, and individual socio-demographic factors (income, age, gender, ethnicity) all play an important role. In the Netherlands, 'living labs' have been created across Dutch cities to enable social scientists to work with citizens to design innovative approaches to cycling infrastructure. There have also been important methodological innovations, with researchers able to use GPS within smartphones or apps such as Strava to access 'ride history data', and examine the impact that cycling infrastructure or traffic levels, for example, have on cyclists' decision-making. Rachel Aldred, an expert on transport, has conducted research on ways to make cycling more accessible in UK cities such as London. Working directly with local governments across the country, she has drawn upon the social sciences to develop insights into a range of emerging pro-cycling policies, from the design of segregated cycle paths to Low Traffic Neighbourhoods (LTNs), which limit motorized through-traffic in residential areas.

Malaria

Around 250 million people suffer from malaria and around 600,000 die each year according to WHO. Addressing global health issues is not just a challenge for medical science; social scientists can also make a difference. Malaria prevention and control involve complex social challenges. Community participation, socio-economic status, and the design of health systems all play a role in incidence, prevalence, and mortality rates.

Across Sub-Saharan Africa, for example, malaria rates are also influenced by factors such as human migration, civil unrest, and conflict.

One of the most important social science findings to shape malaria response has come from Jessica Cohen and Pascaline Dupas, of Harvard and Stanford respectively, who set out to test whether making bed nets available for free rather than charging a nominal fee would make a difference to uptake and use. Based on an RCT with pregnant women in Kenya, they offered discounts of both 90 and 100 per cent of market price, discovering that uptake was 60 percentage points higher when the price was zero compared to when it was $0.60, and that those who accessed them for free still used them properly. These findings have transformed the practice of malaria response around the world, leading to the distribution of millions of bed nets at zero cost, with the UK's Foreign, Commonwealth and Development Office citing the study to call for the abolition of user fees for health products and service in poor countries.

Child literacy

There are significant disparities in educational attainment across young people from different socio-economic backgrounds. One important aspect of this is literacy. Education studies is an interdisciplinary field that aims to understand how people learn and develop through their lives, which has made significant and impactful contributions to improving child literacy. Education scholar Cathy Nutbrown has dedicated her career to researching children's early literacy and development, especially in a pre-school environment for children aged 3–5. Through this research, she has developed tools to support early childhood literacy. One of her observations is that children's learning is shaped by their everyday experiences, and that parents have an important role to play, including through making ordinary experiences like shopping, rhymes, and songs into learning opportunities.

Through this research, she developed a framework called ORIM (Opportunities, Recognition, Interaction, and Model) with her colleague Peter Hannon, which is based on the idea that there are four main ways in which parents can help their children's literacy development. 'Opportunities' relate to turning daily experience of life, such as play or going for a walk, into learning opportunities. 'Recognition' relates to valuing children's efforts and achievements. 'Interaction' relates to listening and talking to children, and involving them in everyday household tasks. 'Modelling' involves showing how literacy and maths are part of everyday life. By testing the model across schools in the UK, and working with local government, ORIM was refined and has now been rolled out across the country by the Department for Education. Teachers and practitioners now share ORIM with families through home visits and literacy events.

Policing

Social Science

Policing studies is another interdisciplinary field of study that has emerged in order to inform evidence-based policing practices. Clifford Stott, for example, is a social psychologist who has led research on policing and crowd behaviour. Over many years, he has researched practices relating to crowd management at sports events and public protests, using a range of methods, including experiments, interviews, and observation. One of his key findings has been that what matters is the perceived legitimacy of policing practice by the 'crowd'. Engagement and dialogue are usually more effective than fear and intimidation. As a result of this research, Stott has worked closely to change practice and training within the Metropolitan Police and the organizers of international football tournaments, for example, leading to the introduction of Police Liaison Officers who focus on building relationships and dialogue, reducing the likelihood of using force.

Across the USA and Europe, social science has also contributed significantly to understanding race and ethnic disproportionality in policing. Across police practice, there has been a long-standing gap between stop and search, arrest, and incarceration rates across different racial and ethnic groups. In many countries, Black and Minority Ethnic (BME) groups have faced disproportionately high rates of stop and search, for example. Researchers Lara Vomfell and Neil Stewart, for example, have used data from 36,000 searches by 1,100 police officers to understand the causes of stereotyping that lead to disproportionality in stop and search in the UK. They have highlighted two key officer-level determinants: the ethnic composition of criminal suspects that officers regularly interact with and the ethnic composition of the areas that they patrol; as well as an important force-level determinant: the over-patrolling of minority areas. Research such as this has contributed to shaping wider research and policy guidance by the Home Office in the UK, and the Office of Justice Programs in the United States, for example, both of which now record and monitor data relating to disproportionality in policing.

Collaborating with government, business, and society

One way to design research for impact is to engage in research collaboration. Many university researchers today build research collaborations with non-academic organizations from across government, business, and society. Involving research-users in research design can be helpful at different stages of the research process: identifying relevant questions, accessing data, and disseminating or implementing findings. In some types of research—such as studies that test interventions—collaboration may be indispensable. As we have seen above, education researchers often need to work with schools and universities, and international development researchers often need to work with UN agencies or NGOs. However, collaboration also comes with challenges, including needing clear alignment on expectations relating to, for example, funding, allocation of responsibilities, and who owns the resulting intellectual property.

To support collaboration, many universities have developed 'engagement' teams, enabling social scientists to access advice and support to work with business, government, the third sector, community organizations, and the public. Engagement can take many forms, involving collaborators as co-investigators, end-users of research, advisers, or funders.

Business engagement may involve a spectrum of knowledge exchange activities—from data-sharing to secondments and placements. However, a particular focus often relates to 'innovation'. Innovation is simply about developing solutions to problems, often by creating a new product. Innovation is a process, and is sometimes conceived of as having four parts: identifying a problem, proposing a solution to that problem, piloting and iterating that solution, and then prototyping the solution. Sometimes this leads to opportunities to commercialize the resulting product, including through patenting, licensing, or forming a spin-out company. Innovation is common in the natural sciences, and it is gradually emerging in the social sciences. For example, Xiaolan Fu led research that resulted in a database examining outcomes for all UK start-ups in the technology sector over a 10-year period. Based on this research, she was able to create an AI-generated model for predicting the value of new tech start-ups. Based on these insights, she created her own spin-out company called OxValue.AI, which offers a valuation tool to determine the commercial value of new technologies. The tool is intended to be used by entrepreneurs to enable them to raise investment, by international organizations involved in technology transfer, national governments to improve GDP accounting, and global corporations for mergers and acquisitions.

Policy engagement involves interacting with people and organizations involved in public affairs. Social science insights can be especially useful for public policy as a source of evidence to inform and legitimate policy design. The work of academics is especially valued because of its perceived independence and objectivity within an environment that is usually shaped by political interests. Policy engagement may include working with activists, parliamentary inquiries, political parties, pressure groups, local and central government, and international organizations. Knowledge exchange may take place through workshops, attending non-academic events, private meetings, or e-mail exchanges. Many academics who successfully navigate public policy do so on the basis of building and maintaining a network of trusted contacts. One key aspect of influencing policy-makers is to repackage research findings in ways that are accessible and succinct—policy briefs, opinion pieces, executive summaries, slide decks, for example, can help summarize key insights. One of the challenges of policy engagement is to avoid instrumentalization, with some policy-makers inevitably valuing academics as a means to legitimate pre-existing political positions.

In my own research on refugee protection, I have gradually built a network of contacts across UN agencies, governments, and NGOs. This has frequently opened opportunities for me to share research at multi-stakeholder meetings at venues such as the UN General Assembly or the US State Department. Policy engagement has enabled me to understand the priorities of policy-makers, identify interesting research questions, share research findings, and influence refugee policies around the world. One of the key areas I have worked on is the right to work for refugees. I have drawn upon research undertaken around the world to try to influence government policies in countries as diverse as Jordan, Colombia, and Uganda. My key takeaway is that policy engagement can be rewarding and contribute to better outcomes. However, it can also be time-consuming, involve navigating complex political interests, and the final results are often outside your control. Policy engagement requires realistic expectations that the influence of your research is likely to be just one influence among many in shaping policy and practice.

Community engagement involves input from people affected by the outcomes of the research, and usually aims to include them as partners within the research process. Community is a broad concept, which may be defined in relation to place (geographical location), practice (shared activity), or identity (e.g. ethnicity, age, or social status). Community engagement often involves working collaboratively with communities in ways that enable them to feel informed, consulted, and involved throughout the research process. They might help come up with research questions, be involved in data collection, or support with interpreting research findings. Depending on the focus of the research, collaborators might include patients, students, parents, teachers, doctors, prisoners, sports coaches, gang members, or local residents. One of the challenges of community-engaged research is making the research process accessible to partners who may have relatively little social science research training. Sometimes this involves investing time and resources into building local capacity for community engaged research. To take an example, social policy expert Lucie Cluver led collaborative research to address child abuse in South Africa, aiming to create and test interventions that could work in townships and local villages. Working with UN agencies and the South African government, her team trained research assistants from the communities, who could build and maintain the trust needed to explore sensitive and sometimes taboo topics with the wider community.

Participatory approaches and co-design

An important group of people implicated in social science research are the research subjects—whether patients (in health research), students (in education research), migrants (in migration studies), or victims or perpetrators of crime (in criminology), for example. How can we include research subjects—who are also potential beneficiaries of the research—within the co-production of research? Participatory Action Research (PAR) has often been highlighted as a means to facilitate a role for subject populations. PAR involves researchers and participants working together to build a shared understand of a particular social challenge, and then iteratively co-designing research that can identify relevant insights or solutions. One of the challenges with PAR is that it often takes place in a context of unequal power relations between researchers and research subjects, and requires significant investment of time and resources to build capacity for meaningful engagement. Nevertheless, it can be an extremely valuable means to improve the ethical legitimacy, quality, and relevance of research.

British academic Robert Chambers was one of the founding figures of participatory research. Working within development studies, he argued that the poor should be taken into account in development research and practice. He suggested that there was a need to move beyond the binary division of researcher/researched or provider/beneficiary, and that development should 'put the last first'. From a research perspective, he showed that communities often have different priorities and categories from researchers, and that the researcher's external categories should not be imposed, but that research and practice should emerge through dialogue. Chambers's approach has been critiqued for under-theorizing the role of power, both in the asymmetrical relationship between researcher and community, and in terms of whose voices 'count' in the research.

Across the social sciences, PAR has grown beyond Chambers's initial ideas, proposing that research and action should include communities affected by that research. Central to this can be the goal of prioritizing experiential knowledge in addressing social problems. People with relevant lived experience should, from this perspective, be co-producers of knowledge. PAR has been informed by ideas drawn from feminist theory and critical race theory, which have long argued that lived experience and situated knowledge (understanding related to context), especially that of historically marginalized groups, should be valued within knowledge production. One of the key ideas here is the slogan 'nothing about us without us', commonly used in the disability movement. In seeking to value expertise beyond the academy, PAR is also committed to action, and production of practical knowledge that can serve the interests of marginalized people and lead to progressive social transformation.

In education studies, for example, researchers Anne Galletta and Maria Elena Torre have included the perspectives of school-age young people in all stages of their work. When examining the effects of school closures in urban USA, they recruited African American students as co-researchers. They facilitated youth participation within the research, by allowing young people to document their experiences in a range of ways including through poetry, drama, and writing. The idea of including young people from affected communities as peer researchers is something used in a growing array of research with implications for children and youth. It offers many benefits in terms of access, insight, and also inspiring communities to engage in research and action, but also entails many ethical challenges, especially when working with potentially vulnerable populations.

It is possible to think about research as existing on a *'participation spectrum'* (Figure 4). At one end of the spectrum is researcher-led research, in which external researchers design and lead the research and communities are simply research subjects. Then there is research in which affected communities are involved selectively in some stages of the research, such as agenda-setting, identifying questions, or assisting with data collection. Then there is co-designed research in which communities are collaborators on all or most stages of the research. Then at the far right of the spectrum is research in which affected communities lead at all stages of the research and the role of external researchers is primarily one of support and facilitation.

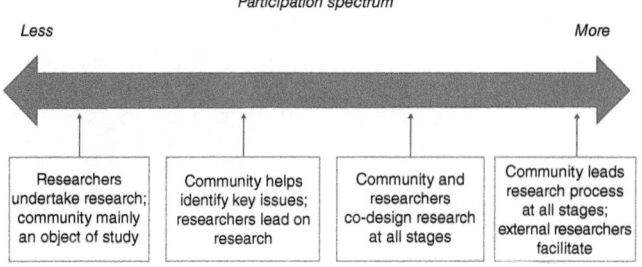

4. Participation spectrum.

Within my own research on refugee protection, I have gradually moved across this spectrum from left to right. Most of my early research was researcher-led, and I designed the research and led at all stages, with input from people with lived experience of displacement being relatively limited. Then, through a programme called the Refugee Economies Programme, colleagues and I started to include refugees within parts of the research process, including as research assistants and peer researchers. Most recently, I co-founded the Refugee-Led Research Hub, which adopts a much more radically participatory approach, supporting people with lived experience of displacement to lead at all stages of the research process. It mainly limits the role of 'external' researchers to facilitation and capacity-building, with some elements of co-design. This approach to research design is rewarding because it builds research capacity among those most affected by the research and leads to research that matters to those communities.

Chapter 6
The future of social science

In recent years, there have been major advances in the social sciences. Significant innovations have been made in the ways researchers seek to understand human behaviour. Many of the most cutting-edge breakthroughs have come from working across disciplines, including by transcending traditional boundaries between the social and the natural sciences. Two of the most influential trends of the 21st century have been behavioural science and human data science, increasingly used not only within universities but also by business and government. A growing proportion of research is now challenge-led, seeking to advance understanding and find practical solutions to 'grand challenges' from climate to public health, in ways that call for social scientists to find effective ways to work collaboratively with natural scientists and humanities scholars. Alongside these trends, there is a renewed reflection on power within the social sciences, critically examining who gets to shape the future of social science. There has also been a welcome turn towards equality, diversity, and inclusion within the social sciences. In this chapter I explore these trends and what they mean for the future production of social knowledge.

Behavioural science

Over the past 40 years, there has been a rapidly growing behavioural science revolution, which has transformed the face of social science. Behavioural scientists generally borrow from economics and psychology to explain and influence people's behaviour. The starting point for behavioural science (or 'behavioural economics') is the view that people are not 'rational' in the way traditionally assumed by economics and much of social science. Acting rationally means weighing up different alternatives, using the information available and choosing the one that maximizes 'utility' (happiness and satisfaction). This rationality assumption is useful because it enables decision-making to be understood as the result of resource constraints (time, money, information). But it is an oversimplification that cannot make sense of the fact that people are often emotional, inconsistent, or seemingly erratic in their choices. Business, for example, has long known that people often pay more for an identical item which has a particular brand on it, whether clothing, breakfast cereal, or pain medication.

People's actions do not always align with their intentions. The rational actor model cannot account for the role that psychological or environmental factors play in shaping behaviour. Instead, behavioural science tries to makes sense of the many ways in which people are 'predictably irrational'—their biases and mental shortcuts.

Behavioural science looks inductively at how people actually behave, when psychological or environmental factors vary. Methodologically, it uses a whole range of social science methods to understand this, including qualitative methods, surveys, the analysis of large datasets, and experiments. Theoretically, behavioural science aims to explain a 'behaviour' (people's decisions), based on the combination of two sets of variables: 'choice environment' (the choices that are presented, and the ways in which they are presented), and 'psychological attributes' (psychologically based tendencies, e.g. a bias). Behavioural science has revealed a whole series of 'biases' (or effects) that influence behaviour when faced with a given set of choices.

American economists Daniel Kahneman and Amos Tversky's work is often viewed as foundational in behavioural science. Based on experiments, they developed 'Prospect Theory', which reveals that people value loss more highly than gain. For example, for some people the pain of losing $25 could only be compensated by the pleasure of gaining $50. They also identified an 'Anchoring Effect', whereby people's decisions are disproportionately influenced by the first piece of information they receive, even if it is arbitrary or irrelevant. The researchers asked people to spin a roulette wheel rigged to land on either '10' or '65'. They then asked them to estimate the number of African countries that were members of the United Nations. Those who landed on 10 estimated on average that there were 25 member countries; those who landed on 65 estimated 45 countries.

Daniel Kahneman's *Thinking, Fast and Slow* suggests that people have two different systems for processing information. System 1 is fast, automatic, and susceptible to environmental influences; System 2 processing is slow, reflective, and takes into account long-term goals and intentions. When situations are complex, immediate, or overwhelming, System 1 processing takes over decision-making. This type of decision-making relies upon 'heuristics' (mental short-cuts) rather than deep, thoughtful reflection. This often leads to choices that appear irrational in relation to an individual's own interests.

Building on these ideas, Cass Sunstein and Richard Thaler developed 'nudge theory' as a means to shape people's behaviour by influencing their System 1 responses. A 'nudge' simply alters the environment in such a way as to favour a particular, desired decision. Sunstein and Thaler define it as an intervention that influences 'people's behaviour in a predictable way without forbidding any options or significantly changing economic incentives'. They show the important role of '*defaults*'—whereby a given choice (such as selecting a vegan food option or organ donation) is presented as the norm and requires 'opt-out' as influencing behaviour. In 2012 the UK government's so-called Nudge Unit drew upon these insights to make pensions opt-out instead of opt-in, leading to hundreds of thousands more people saving for their retirement. Alternatively, '*peer effects*' can change decision-making because people are inclined to follow group norms. These observations have led to governments and businesses around the world creating behavioural science units called 'nudge units'. Many shops engage in product placement; locating sweets or fruit near to the check-out counter can make a difference to consumer choice. Or to encourage vaccinations, governments often use nudges such as reminder text messages or pro-social messaging that reminds people of their wider responsibility to others. Nudges have been used to encourage 'better' choices in areas as diverse as vaccination, savings, exercise, diet, charitable giving, poverty alleviation, climate change mitigation, and discrimination prevention.

Since this early work, researchers have revealed a whole series of mechanisms that shape behaviour, which have been tested through experimental research and used by business and government. George Davis and Elena Serrano summarize eight different behavioural effects from the literature, and illustrate their relevance to the food industry. (1) *Environmental cue effect*—anything in the environment that changes behaviour (e.g. proximity, smell, portion size, packaging background music, lighting). (2) *Default effect*—a standard option that is easily accessible (e.g. a 'combo meal' or something that is easily accessed compared to alternatives). (3) *Framing effect*—how choices are presented: a positive frame will emphasize the positive aspects of a choice (e.g. positive connections with health and fitness); a negative frame will emphasize negative dimensions of a choice (e.g. health warnings relating to junk food). (4) *Ambiguity effect*—how people tend to choose options where known outcomes are favoured over uncertain outcomes (e.g. food choices often select certainty over taste over uncertain negative impact on health). (5) *Confirmation effect*—how people tend to seek information that confirms their preconceptions (e.g. if someone likes dark chocolate, they will be receptive to information that shows that its iron content offers health benefits). (6) *Loss aversion effect*—placing greater value on something you own or risk losing compared to the equivalent gain (e.g. people with high loss aversion may be more likely to make repeat food choices). (7) *Decision fatigue effect*—how the quality of decision-making declines, the more decisions have been made (e.g. people being overwhelmed by long menus with lots of options). (8) *Projection bias effect*—how people overestimate their future abilities and will power and underestimate the effects of future stimulant factors, such as pleasant smells or sights (e.g. assuming they can easily go on a diet or exercise regime in the future).

These types of effects have been revealed by social scientists, often using experimental methods. But they have also been applied to the real world, and many companies invest large amounts of money in the application of behavioural science to predict and influence consumer behaviour. When a business highlights 'best sellers' they are appealing to peer effects. When they highlight that there has been a price reduction ('was $99 ... now $49') they are drawing upon an anchoring effect, whereby people use the first piece of information they hear as a reference point. When the 'special offer' is foregrounded in advertising, the default effect is being deployed. These ideas have also been useful for public policy. By changing people's 'choice architecture', governments can alter behaviour in ways that are better for society. For example, if a government wants more people to use bicycles rather than cars, they might use nudges such as providing better and closer bike parking than is available for cars. The important point about nudges is that they do not rely on either changing the rules or on offering monetary incentives—but they can still have significant influence. While some have questioned the ethics of 'social engineering', especially in the hands of business, the behavioural turn represents a huge advance in how we understand, and can influence, human behaviour.

Human data science

Another recent trend is human data science, which aims to extract meaning from and interpret data, particularly from large datasets, of significant volume, velocity, and variety. The 'Big Data Revolution' is often used to refer to the way in which data produced in the internet have created new research opportunities. New datasets, relating to consumer or citizen choices, have been created by people's use of the internet because whenever people use the internet, they leave a digital footprint. Some of this 'big data' has the potential to offer extraordinary insights into human behaviour and society—in areas such as people's gambling habits, charitable donations, dating lives, investment choices, and civic preferences. Translating this vast quantity of data into usable insights in turn often requires the use of technology, including machine learning and algorithms to organize it. Human data science matters because it can offer useful insights for businesses, policy-makers, and regulatory bodies on the determinants of customer, citizen, and employee behaviour. It also allows social scientists to undertake empirical research without interfering with people's lives through experiments or interviews, for example.

Computer scientists have created new ways of collecting and analysing big data which have profound implications for social science. And social scientists in turn have been developing new techniques for collating and interpreting big data, including by using machine learning for measurement, prediction, and causal inference. Machine learning is a branch of artificial intelligence (AI), developed for analysing big data using algorithms. Machine-learning algorithms are automated and 'learn' from the data. They recognize patterns in datasets, clustering and classifying the data, to build models based on these patterns.

Data from the internet come in many forms, including data from social networks, blogs, and websites, whether textual or visual.

There are also transactional data relating to people's online consumption choices, and data produced by the internet of things (data recording devices placed in homes, white goods, cars, and medical devices), all of which offer insights into behaviour. The challenge is making sense of this data. Human data science has created a range of techniques, to retrieve data, most notably through 'web scraping'. These include using application programming interfaces (APIs), web services that allow direct retrieval of data. *Google Correlate*, for example, offers data relating to Google searches including co-occurrences of keyword searches. Meanwhile, there are techniques to translate text derived from the internet into organized, quantifiable data, known as 'natural language processing', which can be enhanced through machine learning. 'Sentiment analysis' has emerged to make sense of the opinions and emotions within human language. It uses semantics and taxonomies to code for positive or negative meanings in Twitter (now called X) or Facebook posts, for example. Such approaches have been used, for instance, to understand, and explain variation in, public opinion on important political issues from migration to climate change.

Many social scientists use a software programming language (and related software) called Python to analyse big data. Python allows social scientists to design algorithms to undertake analysis of big data, and offers ways to organize and present the resulting analysis. To take an example from international relations, big data methods have been used to explain states' ratification of international human rights and environmental treaties over a 50-year period. Given the huge amount of data involved, covering 193 countries and more than 80 treaties, researchers Alexandros Tokhi and Christian Rauh designed a web-scraping algorithm developed using Python to extract data from the existing United Nations Treaty Collection Database, gathering and organizing around 140,000 observations, in ways that would be impossible based on human observation. Meanwhile, web-scraping techniques have been used by

Benjamin Edelman et al. to analyse postings to online accommodation-sharing platforms, revealing that people with African American names are 16 per cent less likely to be accepted relative to identical guests with distinctively white names. Human data science techniques were especially important in the context of the COVID-19 pandemic. Big data techniques were applied to predict risk, examine vaccination patterns, and monitor public compliance with government policy.

Big data therefore offers a range of transformative opportunities, but also presents challenges. Ensuring the data is of high quality requires cleaning, curation, and standardization. Unlike some areas of social science research, there are also technical barriers to entry in terms of learning techniques derived from computer science such as machine learning. AI will introduce further transformative changes beyond current machine-learning techniques. It will change how questions are asked and answered, and create opportunities to outsource research tasks currently undertaken by humans to machines. There will be a need to ensure all social scientists have at least basic AI literacy, including to be able to critically engage with social knowledge that has been produced using AI. Finally, there are also ethical questions. Using data derived from the internet poses questions relating to privacy, especially in areas such as biometrics or personal data, and potential harm. There is evidence that minority populations are disproportionately harmed by algorithmic decision-making in everything from criminal justice to healthcare decision-making.

Working with the natural sciences and the humanities

Interdisciplinary research is changing the face of social science. And interdisciplinarity is no longer simply about working across the social sciences but increasingly about social scientists working with natural scientists and humanities researchers. This is important because it enables researchers to address complex challenges that transcend disciplinary boundaries. It means that research can be 'challenge-led' rather than shaped by the thematic and bureaucratic boundaries of academic disciplines. From climate change to public health and war, the 'grand challenges' of our time necessitate the integration of diverse disciplinary approaches. However, interdisciplinarity is not always easy, as disciplines have different approaches to knowledge production.

The natural sciences are needed to enable a clear understanding of many of the challenges facing our people and planet, as well as many of the scientific and technological interventions that can be effective. What are the technical solutions to the problems we face (*technical*)? The humanities are needed in order to ground our sense of purpose, ethics, and history—to reflect on how we collectively think of 'the good life'. What should we do when faced with these problems (*normative*)? However, the social sciences have an indispensable contribution to make by providing insights into human behaviour, and how it can be understood, explained, and influenced for the better. What is going to be effective to change people's behaviour to get them to adopt the technical solutions that lead to the outcomes we value (*behavioural*)? If we can combine these technical, normative, and behavioural insights, we have the possibility to change the world for the better. The challenge is that systematic ways to integrate data from different disciplines are still scarce, requiring creativity and flexibility from researchers.

For example, 'climate science' originally emerged to integrate different disciplines from the natural sciences in order to consider technical questions related to, for example, atmospheric carbon dioxide. However, recognizing the importance of understanding the economic value of resources and the need to qualitatively interpret the behaviour and experiences of people causing and living with the consequences of climate change, 'environmental studies' has flourished as a much broader interdisciplinary way to connect the insights of the natural sciences and the social sciences.

More recently, environmental humanities have emerged as a complement to this work, drawing on historical and cultural reflection on how people relate to and experience climate.

But the question is how can disciplines be integrated? Science communication professor David Pedersen identifies three broad types of interdisciplinary approach. First, a *division of labour*—researchers with strong disciplinary backgrounds assume responsibility for particular aspects of the research process. For example, in a project on the determinants of child mental health outcomes, a geneticist might focus on understanding hereditary factors while a sociologist might examine the role of the child's upbringing. Second, working within an *interdisciplinary field*—researchers work within a sub-field with a set of shared research principles (e.g. gender studies, refugee studies, or area studies). Third, *in-bound mobility* of researchers from other disciplines into disciplinary research. For example, a medical science research project working on pandemics might include an anthropologist to understand relevant lived experience, or an economics project examining gambling behaviour might include a cognitive neuroscientist to make sense of the role of the brain in decision-making.

Let's examine some examples of global challenges in which social scientists have worked effectively with natural scientists. If we consider *conservation*, natural science can tell us about trends in fish stocks over time. It can offer insights that are physical (ocean temperatures), biogeochemical (e.g. nutrients), or biological (biomass). But, as Isabel Richter and her colleagues point out, social science is needed in order to understand the perspective of community members, including fishers to uncover key societal changes (in fishing practices or river use) that may have influenced trends. Indigenous communities may have traditional ecological knowledge based on lived experience. One of the challenges is how to meaningfully integrate and compare these different types of data. To do so, researchers have transformed data on community perceptions into a so-called Likert scale (a range that represents qualitative data on a quantifiable scale, e.g. 'strong improvement', 'improvement', 'no change', 'decline', 'strong decline').

In the context of *epidemiology*, to address the COVID-19 pandemic governments relied upon not only scientific advice, but also input from social scientists. In the UK, the Scientific Advisory Group for Emergencies (SAGE) provided scientific and technical advice to support government decision-making, but also recruited social scientists to align human behaviour with the recommendations of public health experts. Jay Van Bavel et al. show how social scientists were able to offer government decision-makers a whole series of important insights. For example, 'identity effects'—a shared sense of identity or purpose can be encouraged by addressing the public in collective terms and by urging 'us' to act for the common good. 'Leadership effects'—messaging from people (e.g. religious or community leaders) that are credible to different audiences to share public health messages can be effective. 'Peer effects'—norms of pro-social behaviour (e.g. hand-washing or mask-wearing) are more effective if there is a perception that other people from within your group hold the same pro-social values, and that esteem comes with conformity and shame with non-conformity.

If we turn to *neuroscience*, improved understanding of how the brain works is transformative for social science, shaping how we think about themes like rationality, emotion, cooperation, negotiation, and motivation. As the nature–nurture divide collapses, so it becomes crucial to understand how the cognitive and social worlds interact and influence one another. Socio-economic status has been found to affect brain-functioning in areas from emotional response to empathy. This is because people's social experiences of relative deprivation or privilege actually change the physiology of their brains, and hence their thoughts, feelings, and behaviours. Cognitive anthropology examines how the biological and social interact. For example, it has explored how religious and other rituals shape group cohesion, including by examining the impact on biological factors such as sensory arousal. Martha Newson has looked at how intra-group bonding takes place among football fans, including by exploring the effects of football fan rituals on biological indicators (e.g. heart rates and hormone levels) and, in turn, on behaviour (e.g. hooliganism and violence).

There are also important intersections with the humanities. The humanities offer insight into people's lived experiences, past and present, including how these are documented in literature, visual art, and narrative storytelling. Discourses, narratives, and representations are central to the humanities. History is closely intertwined with the social sciences, and most social sciences include a historical perspective—albeit that social scientists are often more interested in identifying systematic patterns from the past. Philosophy underpins a significant proportion of social science theory, reflection on methodology, and ethical and normative approaches to thinking about the social and political worlds. New areas of intersection are emerging such as environmental humanities and legal humanities. The humanities have also offered important insights for social scientists in terms of how to work across cultures, appreciate context, value diverse approaches to knowledge production, and recognize the relationship between power and knowledge.

Equality, diversity, and inclusion in the social sciences

Social science has historically been disproportionately shaped by white, male researchers in Europe and North America. A significant amount of early social scientific knowledge also builds on the legacies of colonialism. And, as I write, far too few university professors in the social sciences come from diverse backgrounds. This impoverishes social science because it excludes valuable perspectives and lived experiences. However, social science has also made notable contributions to address racism, sexism, heteronormativity, and other sources of oppression. And it is also uniquely well placed to disrupt patterns of exclusion and identify opportunities for societal transformation and social justice. Achieving this needs to begin with creating an approach to social science that is inclusive, diverse, and embraces a plurality of perspectives, including ideas and approaches from across the spectrum of the social sciences. Practical measures for achieving this need to include embedding equality, diversity, and inclusion considerations in research proposals, valuing the role that lived experience can play in shaping social inquiry, and expanding access to graduate-level social science training for aspiring researchers from historically under-represented backgrounds.

An increasing body of research recognizes that social science has predominantly been a history of ideas developed by white men. One response to that has been to re-centre marginalized voices within social science debates. For example, scholars have revisited the history of international political thought to give visibility to neglected ideas developed by female international relations scholars during the 20th century, while political scientists have undertaken research on the history of political thought by Sub-Saharan African scholars.

Across the social sciences there has been a growing focus on decolonizing knowledge, based on recognition that a significant part of dominant knowledge is built upon the legacies of Empire. Across law, sociology, and economics, many supposedly 'universal' ideas—from thinking about the Global North/Global South to the dissemination of common law frameworks—are intertwined with the legacies of Empire. The decolonizing movement gained momentum alongside the Rhodes Must Fall campaign beginning at the University of Cape Town in 2015, and the murder of George Floyd in 2020, which triggered the Black Lives Matter movement. Decolonizing is a complex idea aimed at 'undoing' the power relations and structures of exclusion created by colonialism. For the social sciences, this means producing and disseminating knowledge that is not dependent on Eurocentric epistemologies, that challenges hierarchies of knowledge creation, and re-centres the voices and perspectives of people marginalized by the legacies of colonialism.

These ideas build upon earlier influential ideas. For example, Palestinian-American academic Edward Said's *Orientalism* (1978) highlighted the role of discriminatory prejudice within Western cultural representations of the Middle East. Egyptian economist Samir Amin's concept 'Eurocentrism' shows how Western thought centres and privileges European perspectives, judging other cultures through a European lens, in ways that reinforce hierarchies and domination. Francophone Afro-Caribbean intellectual Frantz Fanon's *Black Skin, White Masks* (1952) reveals how Black people are often compelled to performatively reproduce the language and behaviour of white culture. Since the inception of these ideas, a large body of thought has emerged in areas such as critical race theory, using a range of theoretical and methodological tools to reveal the ways in which social scientific knowledge is sometimes imbued with structural racism.

Equality, diversity, and inclusion (EDI) also requires diversifying who has the opportunity to become a social scientist. Who gets to train as a social scientist and access PhD programmes? Who gets to be a university professor in the social sciences? To what extent are there adequate pipelines to support people from Black and Minoritized Ethnic—or 'global majority'—backgrounds to access graduate training and become successful academics? In the UK, while around 3 per cent of PhD students were Black in 2019 (slightly less than the overall proportion of Black British people in the UK), only 1.2 per cent of government (UKRI) PhD scholarships were awarded to Black or Mixed Black students and just 1 per cent of professors were from those backgrounds, according to HESA. In the USA, Black faculty were just 6 per cent of all faculty (despite making up 13 per cent of the population), with 38 per cent having tenure (compared to 47 per cent of white faculty), according to the National Center for Education Statistics.

Social science matters because it has the potential to change society. It is therefore crucial that the producers of social scientific knowledge reflect a diverse array of standpoints, positionalities, and lived experiences. Diversity in terms of race, gender, disability, age, sexual orientation, class, and other factors is crucial to ensure that the social sciences flourish. Potential rather than past privilege should define who has the opportunity to create influential social research. And—as we know from almost all organizations—diversity tends to improve performance, contribute to innovation, and create more dynamic and effective teams.

Social science is constantly evolving. As social trends change, opportunities for novel research questions emerge. New technologies, geopolitical change, and the recognition of social injustice provide constant inspiration for creativity. To the social scientist, emerging global challenges represent opportunities for innovation and the possibility to make a difference. The rapidly evolving social science toolbox offers an array of methods and theories for making sense of global challenges.

My hope is that by reading this book, you have been inspired to use some of those tools of social science to make sense of economic, social, and political trends. In an era in which 'truth' is constantly questioned, social science offers a means to judge and contest the validity of claims made by politicians and others in positions of authority. It offers the chance to build new knowledge and leverage progressive social change, whether locally, nationally, or globally.

Opportunities for innovative social science come from working beyond traditional disciplinary boundaries. New opportunities will also emerge from being open to learning across different traditions of social thought. In this book, I have mainly focused on social scientific knowledge that has emerged in Europe and North America. This is because many of the dominant and influential ideas within the social sciences have emerged from universities within those regions. Integrating traditions of social thought from China, India, and across Africa, for example, will enrich social science in the decades to come. There is huge scope to go beyond Western-centric approaches, and to consider what truly 'global social science' could look like.

References

Chapter 1: What is social science?

Buyalskaya, Anastasia, Marcos Gallo, and Colin F. Camerer. 'The golden age of social science'. *Proceedings of the National Academy of Sciences* 118.5 (2021): e2002923118.

McLean, Iain. 'What is social science?' (2018), The British Academy, <https://www.thebritishacademy.ac.uk/blog/what-social-science/>

Comte, Auguste. *A General View of Positivism.* Reeves & Turner, 1880.

Weber, Max, and Stephen Kalberg. *The Protestant Ethic and the Spirit of Capitalism.* Routledge, 2013.

Marx, Karl. *Capital.* Vol. 1. Penguin UK, 2004.

Popper, Karl. *The Logic of Scientific Discovery.* Routledge, 2005.

King, Gary, Robert O. Keohane, and Sidney Verba. *Designing Social Inquiry: Scientific Inference in Qualitative Research.* Princeton University Press, 2021.

Simon, Herbert Alexander. *Models of Bounded Rationality: Empirically Grounded Economic Reason.* Vol. 3. MIT Press, 1997.

Chapter 2: Doing social science

Moravcsik, Andrew. 'The origins of human rights regimes: Democratic delegation in postwar Europe'. *International Organization* 54.2 (2000): 217–52.

Rivera, Lauren A. 'Hiring as cultural matching: The case of elite professional service firms'. *American Sociological Review* 77.6 (2012): 999–1022.

Mazrekaj, Deni, Kristof De Witte, and Sofie Cabus. 'School outcomes of children raised by same-sex parents: Evidence from administrative panel data'. *American Sociological Review* 85.5 (2020): 830–56.

Hill, Austin Bradford. 'The environment and disease: Association or causation?' *Journal of the Royal Society of Medicine* 58.5 (1965): 295–300.

Feyerabend, Paul. *Against Method: Outline of an Anarchistic Theory of Knowledge.* Verso Books, 1975 (2020).

Malinowski, Bronislaw. *Argonauts of the Western Pacific: An Account of Native Enterprise and Adventure in the Archipelagoes of Melanesian New Guinea [1922/1994].* Routledge, 2013.

Geertz, Clifford. *The Interpretation of Cultures.* Vol. 5019. Basic Books, 1973.

Ricoeur, Paul. *Oneself as Another.* University of Chicago Press, 1992.

Foucault, Michel. *The History of Sexuality: 1: The Will to Knowledge.* Penguin UK, 2019.

Ferguson, James. *The Anti-politics Machine: 'Development,' Depoliticization, and Bureaucratic Power in Lesotho.* University of Minnesota Press, 1994.

Campbell, David. *Politics Without Principle: Sovereignty, Ethics, and the Narratives of the Gulf War.* Lynne Rienner Publishers, 1993.

Weldes, Jutta, ed. *Cultures of Insecurity: States, Communities, and the Production of Danger.* Vol. 14. University of Minnesota Press, 1999.

Chapter 3: Theories and concepts

Bhattacherjee, Anol. *Social Science Research: Principles, Methods, and Practices.* CreateSpace Independent Publishing Platform, 2012.

Durkheim, Émile. *Emile Durkheim on Morality and Society.* University of Chicago Press, 1973.

Kuhn, Thomas S. *The Structure of Scientific Revolutions.* University of Chicago Press (1962), 2: 90.

Becker, Gary S. 'A theory of marriage: Part II'. *Journal of Political Economy* 82.2, Part 2 (1974): S11–S26.

Andreoni, James. 'Giving with impure altruism: Applications to charity and Ricardian equivalence'. *Journal of Political Economy* 97.6 (1989): 1447–58.

Fearon, James D., and David D. Laitin. 'Ethnicity, insurgency, and civil war'. *American Political Science Review* 97.1 (2003): 75–90.

Bourdieu, Pierre. *Outline of a Theory of Practice.* The new social theory reader. Routledge, 2020: 80–6.

Giddens, Anthony. *New Rules of Sociological Method*. Stanford University Press, 1993.

Wendt, Alexander. 'Anarchy is what states make of it: The social construction of power politics'. *International Organization* 46.2 (1992): 391–425.

Hardt, Michael, and Antonio Negri. *Empire*. Harvard University Press, 2001.

Gramsci, Antonio. *Prison Notebooks*. Vol. 2. Columbia University Press, 2011.

Cardoso, Fernando Henrique, and Enzo Faletto. *Dependency and Development in Latin America*. University of California Press, 1979.

Escobar, Arturo. *Encountering Development: The Making and Unmaking of the Third World*. Vol. 1. Princeton University Press, 2011.

Butler, Judith. *Frames of War: When Is Life Grievable?* Verso Books, 2016.

Doty, Roxanne Lynn. *Imperial Encounters: The Politics of Representation in North–South Relations*. Vol. 5. University of Minnesota Press, 1996.

Tversky, Amos, and Daniel Kahneman. 'Judgment under uncertainty: Heuristics and biases. Biases in judgments reveal some heuristics of thinking under uncertainty'. *Science* 185.4157 (1974): 1124–31.

Olson Jr, Mancur. *The Logic of Collective Action: Public Goods and the Theory of Groups, with a New Preface and Appendix*. Vol. 124. Harvard University Press, 1971.

Ostrom, Elinor. *Governing the Commons: The Evolution of Institutions for Collective Action*. Cambridge University Press, 1990.

Kant, Immanuel. *Perpetual Peace and Other Essays*. Hackett Publishing, 1795/1983.

Barnett, Michael, and Raymond Duvall. 'Power in international politic'. *International Organization* 59.1 (2005): 39–75.

Collier, Paul, and Anke Hoeffler. 'Greed and grievance in civil war'. *Oxford Economic Papers* 56.4 (2004): 563–95.

Chapter 4: Methods and methodologies

Geertz, Clifford. 'Deep hanging out'. *The New York Review of Books* 45.16 (1998): 69–72.

Evans-Pritchard, Edward Evan. *The Nuer: A Description of the Modes of Livelihood and Political Institutions of a Nilotic People*. Oxford University Press, 1940.

Nader, Laura. 'Up the anthropologist: Perspectives gained from studying up' (1972). <https://eric.ed.gov/?id=ED065375>

Shore, Chris, and Susan Wright, eds. *Anthropology of Policy: Perspectives on Governance and Power*. Routledge, 2003.

Saunders, Benjamin, et al. 'Saturation in qualitative research: Exploring its conceptualization and operationalization'. *Quality & Quantity* 52 (2018): 1893–907.

Richards, Paul. *Fighting for the Rain Forest: War, Youth & Resources in Sierra Leone*. James Currey Ltd, 1996.

Willis, Paul. *Learning to Labour: How Working Class Kids Get Working Class Jobs*. Routledge, 2017.

Autesserre, Séverine. *The Trouble with the Congo: Local Violence and the Failure of International Peacebuilding*. Vol. 115. Cambridge University Press, 2010.

George, Alexander L., and Andrew Bennett. *Case Studies and Theory Development in the Social Sciences*. MIT Press, 2005.

Tannenwald, Nina. 'The nuclear taboo: The United States and the normative basis of nuclear non-use'. *International Organization* 53.3 (1999): 433–68.

Collier, David. 'Understanding process tracing'. *PS: Political Science & Politics* 44.4 (2011): 823–30.

Salganik, Matthew J. *Bit by Bit: Social Research in the Digital Age*. Princeton University Press, 2019.

Chapter 5: How social science can change the world

Bakewell, Oliver. 'Research beyond the categories: The importance of policy irrelevant research into forced migration'. *Journal of Refugee Studies* 21.4 (2008): 432–53.

Smith, Katherine E., et al. *The Impact Agenda: Controversies, Consequences and Challenges*. Policy Press, 2020.

Patalay, Praveetha, and Emla Fitzsimons. 'Development and predictors of mental ill-health and wellbeing from childhood to adolescence'. *Social Psychiatry and Psychiatric Epidemiology* 53 (2018): 1311–23.

Chetty, Raj, et al. 'Income segregation and intergenerational mobility across colleges in the United States'. *The Quarterly Journal of Economics* 135.3 (2020): 1567–633.

Bales, Kevin. *Disposable People: New Slavery in the Global Economy, Updated with a New Preface*. University of California Press, 2012.

Baseler, Travis, et al. 'Can redistribution change policy views? Aid and attitudes toward refugees in Uganda'. Working paper 645. Center for Global Development, 2023.

Lee, Barrett A., Kimberly A. Tyler, and James D. Wright. 'The new homelessness revisited'. *Annual Review of Sociology* 36 (2010): 501–21.

Alkire, Sabina, and James Foster. 'Counting and multidimensional poverty measurement'. *Journal of Public Economics* 95.7–8 (2011): 476–87.

Banerjee, Abhijit V., and Esther Duflo. 'The economic lives of the poor'. *Journal of Economic Perspectives* 21.1 (2007): 141–67.

Aldred, Rachel. 'Governing transport from welfare state to hollow state: The case of cycling in the UK'. *Transport Policy* 23 (2012): 95–102.

Avineri, Erel. 'On the use and potential of behavioural economics from the perspective of transport and climate change'. *Journal of Transport Geography* 24 (2012): 512–21.

Handy, Susan, Bert Van Wee, and Maarten Kroesen. 'Promoting cycling for transport: Research needs and challenges'. *Transport Reviews* 34.1 (2014): 4–24.

Berney, Rachel, ed. *Bicycle Urbanism: Reimagining Bicycle Friendly Cities*. Routledge, 2018.

Cohen, Jessica, and Pascaline Dupas. 'Free distribution or cost-sharing? Evidence from a randomized malaria prevention experiment.' *The Quarterly Journal of Economics* 125.1 (2010): 1–45.

Nutbrown, Cathy. *Threads of Thinking: Young Children Learning and the Role of Early Education*. Sage, 2006.

Stott, Clifford, and Steve Reicher. 'How conflict escalates: The inter-group dynamics of collective football crowd violence'. *Sociology* 32.2 (1998): 353–77.

Vomfell, Lara, and Neil Stewart. 'Officer bias, over-patrolling and ethnic disparities in stop and search'. *Nature Human Behaviour* 5.5 (2021): 566–75.

Cluver, Lucie, et al. 'Parenting in a time of COVID-19'. *Lancet* 395 (2020): E64.

Chambers, Robert. *Rural Development: Putting the Last First*. Routledge, 1983/2014.

Rahnema, Majid. 'Participatory action research: The "last temptation of saint" development'. *Alternatives* 15.2 (1990): 199–226.

Galletta, Anne, and María Elena Torre. 'Participatory action research in education'. *Oxford Research Encyclopedia of Education*. Oxford University Press, 2019.

Burns, Janice, et al. *A Short Guide to Community-Based Participatory Action Research*. Healthy City, 2011.

Chapter 6: The future of social science

Tversky, Amos, and Daniel Kahneman. 'Judgment under uncertainty: Heuristics and biases. Biases in judgments reveal some heuristics of thinking under uncertainty'. *Science* 185.4157 (1974): 1124–31.

Kahneman, Daniel. *Thinking, Fast and Slow*. Macmillan, 2011.

Thaler, Richard H., and Cass R. Sunstein. *Nudge: Improving Decisions about Health, Wealth, and Happiness*. Penguin, 2009.

Davis, George C., and Elena L. Serrano. *Food and Nutrition Economics: Fundamentals for Health Sciences*. Oxford University Press, 2016.

Amaturo, Enrica, and Biagio Aragona. 'Methods for big data in social sciences'. *Mathematical Population Studies* 26.2 (2019): 65–8.

Tokh, Alexandrosi and Christian Rauh, 'Big data in the social sciences'. Berlin Social Science Center (2015), <https://wzb.eu/en/publications/wzb-mitteilungen/big-data-in-den-sozialwissenschaften>

Edelman, Benjamin, Michael Luca, and Dan Svirsky. 'Racial discrimination in the sharing economy: Evidence from a field experiment.' *American Economic Journal: Applied Economics* 9.2 (2017): 1–22.

Belenguer, Lorenzo. 'AI bias: Exploring discriminatory algorithmic decision-making models and the application of possible machine-centric solutions adapted from the pharmaceutical industry'. *AI and Ethics* 2.4 (2022): 771–87.

Pedersen, David Budtz. 'Integrating social sciences and humanities in interdisciplinary research'. *Palgrave Communications* 2.1 (2016): 1–7.

Richter, Isabel, et al. 'Building bridges between natural and social science disciplines: A standardized methodology to combine data on ecosystem quality trends'. *Philosophical Transactions of the Royal Society B* 377.1854 (2022): 20210487.

Bavel, Jay J. Van, et al. 'Using social and behavioural science to support COVID-19 pandemic response'. *Nature Human Behaviour* 4.5 (2020): 460–71.

Pinker, Steven. *Language, Cognition, and Human Nature: Selected Articles*. Oxford University Press, 2013.

Ibáñez, Agustín, Lucas Sedeño, and Adolfo M. García, eds. *Neuroscience and Social Science: The Missing Link*. Springer International Publishing, 2017.

Newson, Martha. 'Football, fan violence, and identity fusion'. *International Review for the Sociology of Sport* 54.4 (2019): 431–44.

Said, Edward W. *Orientalism*. Routledge, 1978/2023.

Amin, Samir. *Eurocentrism*. NYU Press, 1989.

Fanon, Frantz. 'Black skin, white masks'. *Social Theory Re-wired*. Routledge, 2016: 394–401.

Bonilla-Silva, Eduardo. 'Rethinking racism: Toward a structural interpretation'. *American Sociological Review* 62.3 (1997): 465–80.

Hunt, Vivian, Dennis Layton, and Sara Prince. 'Diversity matters'. McKinsey & Company 1.1 (2015): 15–29.

Further reading

Chapter 1: What is social science?

There are relatively few great introductions to social science. Textbooks are generally discipline-specific, or focus on qualitative or quantitative methods. An exception to this is Kath Woodward's *Social Sciences: The Big Issues* (2021). One way to engage with the social sciences is to read the 'classics' to understand the history of social scientific thought. These include Max Weber's *The Protestant Ethic and the Spirit of Capitalism* (1880); Karl Marx's *Capital: A Critique of Political Economy*, Vol. 1 (1865); August Comte's *A General View of Positivism* (1848); Adam Smith's *The Wealth of Nations* (1776); Thucydides' *History of the Peloponnesian War* (5th century BC). However, these should be read with an awareness that they are almost exclusively written by European men. Important correctives to this include Judith Butler's *Gender Trouble: Feminism and the Subversion of Identity* (2006), Kimberle Crenshaw's *On Intersectionality* (2014), and Edward Said's *Orientalism* (1978), for example. Another way into social science is to read accessible work by inspiring contemporary social scientists, on themes that interest you. Steven Levitt and Stephen Dubner's *Freakonomics* (2005) offers a great introduction to economics, Kate Fox's *Watching the English* (2004) to anthropology, and Tim Marshall's *The Power of Geography* (2021) to geography. To understand the value of interdisciplinary social science, read popular social science books on topics that interest you. Caroline Criado Perez's *Invisible Women* (2019) for thinking about gender, Thomas Piketty's *Capital in the Twenty-First Century* (2013) for a critique of capitalism, Angela Saini's *Superior* (2019) on the rise of scientific racism, Jonathan Haidt's *The Righteous Mind* (2012) on pro-social behaviour, Danny Dorling's *Injustice: Why Social Inequality Still Persists* (2010) on inequality, or Jared Diamond's *Guns, Germs, and Steel* (1997) to think about social history over the *longue durée*.

Chapter 2: Doing social science

Learning how to 'do' social science is partly about mastering a series of principles, methods, and practices. There are some excellent texts on research design. Anol Bhattacherjee's *Social Science Research* (2012) is a hidden gem. From a positivist perspective, Gary King, Robert Keohane, and Sidney Verba's *Designing Social Inquiry* remains one of the seminal social science research design texts, and has attracted critical engagement. For a broader perspective, *Bryman's Social Research Methods* (2021), co-authored by Alan Bryman with colleagues, offers important insights into how to design social scientific research. One way of understanding social science research design is to read examples of excellent social science by authors that include significant reflection on their own research methods and research design process. Research monographs that have inspired my own reflections on research design include: Jutta Weldes's *Cultures of Insecurity* (1999) on discourse analysis, Nina Tannenwald's *The Nuclear Taboo* (1999) on process tracing, James Ferguson's *The Anti-Politics Machine* (1994) on ethnography, Lamis Abdelaaty's *Discrimination and Delegation* (2021) on mixed methods research design, or Michael Findley and colleagues' *Shell Games* (1994) on experimental methods. To learn about the practice of research design, there is very little better approach than reading social scientists' own accounts of what they actually do.

Chapter 3: Theories and concepts

My approach to social science theory is that no one theoretical approach is inherently better than another. Different approaches have relative strengths and weaknesses. Because social scientists often specialize, there are few textbooks on 'social science theory'. The best way to understand theory is to read examples of how theory is applied by social scientists. On rational choice, Gary Becker's (1974) 'A theory of marriage' argues for the applicability of rational choice to the seemingly most unlikely of contexts, as does Paul Collier and Anke Hoeffler's 'Greed and grievance in civil war' (2004) in looking at even 'ethnic conflict' as driven by rational self-interest. On social constructionism, Alex Wendt's *Social Theory of International Politics* (1998) or Paul Willis's *Learning to Labour* (1977) offer ways to bring to life the interaction of structure and agency in the context of intergovernmental relations and secondary school education respectively. On Marxism, Michael Hardt and Antonio Negri's *Empire* (2001) shows the diversity and applicability of Marxist concepts to contemporary notions of imperialism. On critical theory, Arturo Escobar's *Encountering Development* (2011) or Judith Butler's *Frames of War* (2016) provide applications of the ideas of Michel Foucault and other post-structuralist thinkers. In addition to grand theories, it is worthwhile to read seminal works that have led to key concepts in the social sciences, such as Mancur Olson's *The Logic of Collective Action* (1965), Steven Lukes's *Power* (1974), Charles Tilly's *The Politics of Collective Violence* (2003) on social movements, Pierre Bourdieu's *Outline of a Theory of Practice* (1977), which details his concept of 'habitus', or Anthony's Giddens's *The Constitution of Society* (1984), which outlines the idea of 'structuration'.

Chapter 4: Methods and methodologies

Matthew Salganik's *Bit by Bit: Social Research in the Digital Age* (2019) offers a truly excellent framework for thinking about social science methods, which transcends traditional qualitative–quantitative divides. His focus on observation, asking questions, and experiments can, of course, be critiqued but is a compelling way to divide of the cake of methodological approaches to social science. In terms of qualitative research, Jane Ritchie's *Qualitative Research Practice: A Guide for Social Science Students and Researchers* (2013) is a great introduction written from a UK perspective. Bruce Berg's *Qualitative Research Methods for the Social Sciences* (2017) is one of the best from a US perspective. Process tracing has become one of the most popular qualitative social science methods, and all social scientists should probably read Alexander George and Andrew Bennett's *Case Studies and Theory Development in the Social Sciences* (2005). In terms of quantitative methods, Thomas Black's *Doing Quantitative Research in the Social Sciences: An Integrated Approach to Research Design, Measurement and Statistics* (1999) has also been updated and reissued several times and is clear on basic principles. There are a whole range of quantative method texts that focus variously on mastering data analysis in software packages such as SPSS, Stata, R. On experimental methods,

Renita Coleman's *Designing Experiments for the Social Sciences* (2019) is relatively unique. More generally, Paul Gertler et al.'s *Impact Evaluation in Practice* (2016) published by the World Bank offers an excellent guide to impact evaluation methods, which are widely used in public policy and business as well as universities.

Chapter 5: How social science can change the world

For an overview of the 'impact agenda' in the social sciences, and critiques of that agenda, Katherine Smith et al.'s *The Impact Agenda* (2020) is a useful starting point. The impact agenda has probably been most pronounced in the UK. Reflecting this the Economic and Social Research Council (ESRC) has created a website full of inspiring 'impact case studies', often drawn from its annual social science impact awards. The Academy of Social Science has done similarly. In the USA, J-PAL, for example, has also curated an excellent webpage documenting the impact of its research on policy and practice. These websites are worth looking at to understand the range of pathways that exist for social science impact. But it's also worth reading some of the original research that underlies social impact. For example, Jessica Cohen and Pascaline Dupas's 'Free distribution or cost-sharing? Evidence from a randomized malaria prevention experiment' in *The Quarterly Journal of Economics* (2010) is an excellent methodological example of impact evaluation which has profoundly changed the practice of malaria prevention. The range of examples in the references list for Chapter 5 offers many other good examples of impactful social science for further reading. There is growing interest in Participatory Action Research across the social sciences. For an understanding of early thinking in this area, the Robert Chambers–Majid Rahnema readings listed in the references offer an insight into the strengths and weaknesses of participatory approaches to social science.

Chapter 6: The future of social science

There are lots of accessible and inspiring books about behavioural science, particularly Daniel Kahneman's *Thinking, Fast and Slow* (2011); Richard Thaler's *Nudge: Improving Decision About Health, Wealth, and Happiness* (2008); and Dan Ariely *Predictably Irrational: The Hidden Forces That Shape Our Decisions* (2008). Jay Van Bavel et al.'s *Nature* article in 2020 offers a fascinating insight into how behavioural science shaped the response to the COVID-19 pandemic.

One of the challenges of importing insights from complex technical areas like AI, machine learning, or neuroscience is finding publications that make them accessible for a generalist social science audience. There are a few hidden gems, such as Enrica Amaturo and Biagio Aragona's 'Methods for big data in social sciences' article in *Mathematical Population Studies* (2019), Agustin Ibáñez et al.'s *Neuroscience and Social Science: The Missing Link* (2017), and Isabel Richter et al.'s 'Building bridges between natural and social science disciplines: a standardized methodology to combine data on ecosystem quality trends' in *Philosophical Transactions of the Royal Society* (2022). Steven Pinker's *The Blank Slate* (2002) is an accessible way to start thinking about the complex relationship between 'nature' and 'nurture' in shaping human behaviour and why the social and natural sciences need to work together. In terms of decolonizing social science research, important seminar texts include Samir Amin's *Eurocentrism* (1988) and Frantz Fanon's *The Wretched of the Earth* (1961), while insightful contemporary works include Stefania Fuentes et al.'s *How to Start Decolonising Social Sciences: A Workbook* (2022).

Index

For the benefit of digital users, indexed terms that span two pages (e.g., 52–53) may, on occasion, appear on only one of those pages.

BEHAVIOURAL ECONOMICS
A Very Short Introduction
Michelle Baddeley

Traditionally economists have based their economic predictions on the assumption that humans are super-rational creatures, using the information we are given efficiently and generally making selfish decisions that work well for us as individuals. Economists also assume that we're doing the very best we can possibly do—not only for today, but over our whole lifetimes too. Increasingly, however, the study of behavioural economics is revealing that our lives are not that simple. Instead, our decisions are complicated by our own psychology. Each of us makes mistakes every day. We don't always know what's best for us and, even if we do, we might not have the self-control to deliver on our best intentions. We struggle to stay on diets, to get enough exercise, and to manage our money.

This *Very Short Introduction* explores the reasons why we make irrational decisions; how we decide quickly; why we make mistakes in risky situations; our tendency to procrastinate; and how we are affected by social influences, personality, mood, and emotions. As Michelle Baddeley explains, the implications of understanding the rationale for our own financial behaviour are huge. She concludes by looking forward, to see what the future of behavioural economics holds for us.

CITIZENSHIP
A Very Short Introduction
Richard Bellamy

Interest in citizenship has never been higher. But what does it mean to be a citizen of a modern, complex community? Why is citizenship important? Can we create citizenship, and can we test for it? In this fascinating Very Short Introduction, Richard Bellamy explores the answers to these questions and more in a clear and accessible way. He approaches the subject from a political perspective, to address the complexities behind the major topical issues. Discussing the main models of citizenship, exploring how ideas of citizenship have changed through time from ancient Greece to the present, and examining notions of rights and democracy, he reveals the irreducibly political nature of citizenship today.

> 'Citizenship is a vast subject for a short introduction, but Richard Bellamy has risen to the challenge with aplomb.'
>
> **Mark Garnett, TLS**

www.oup.com/vsi